11702

$16.00

D0387634

DATE DUE

Demco, Inc. 38-293

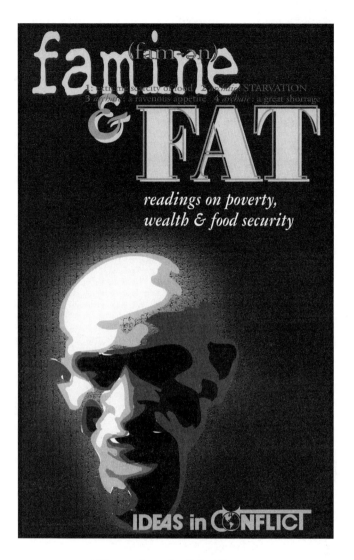

famine

(fam·en)

1 : acute scarcity of food 2 *obsolete* : STARVATION
3 *archaic* : a ravenous appetite 4 *archaic* : a great shortage

& FAT

*readings on poverty,
wealth & food security*

IDEAS in CONFLICT

Marnie J. McCuen

GARY McCUEN
publications inc.

411 Mallalieu Drive
Hudson, Wisconsin 54016
Phone (715) 386-7113

Illustrations and Photo Credits

Bob Lang 100; Barrie Maguire 43; Andrew Singer 79; Dan Wasserman 49.

© 2000 by Gary E. McCuen Publications, Inc.
411 Mallalieu Drive, Hudson, Wisconsin 54016

(715) 386-7113

International Standard Book Number
0-86596-183-2
Printed in the United States of America

CONTENTS

Ideas in Conflict

Introduction

Part I. HUNGRY FOR RELIEF: THE GLOBAL SOUTH, TRADE AND DEBT

REASONING SKILL DEVELOPMENT

These activities may be used as individualized study guides for students in libraries and resource centers or as discussion catalysts in small group and classroom discussions.

IDEAS
in CONFLICT

This series features ideas in conflict on political, social, and moral issues. It presents counterpoints, debates, opinions, commentary, and analysis for use in libraries and classrooms. Each title in the series uses one or more of the following basic elements:

Introductions that present an issue overview giving historic background and/or a description of the controversy.

Counterpoints and debates carefully chosen from publications, books, and position papers on the political right and left to help librarians and teachers respond to requests that treatment of public issues be fair and balanced.

Symposiums and forums that go beyond debates that can polarize and oversimplify. These present commentary from across the political spectrum that reflect how complex issues attract many shades of opinion.

A **global** emphasis with foreign perspectives and surveys on various moral questions and political issues that will help readers to place subject matter in a less culture-bound and ethnocentric frame of reference. In an ever-shrinking and interdependent world, understanding and cooperation are essential. Many issues are global in nature and can be effectively dealt with only by common efforts and international understanding.

Reasoning skill study guides and discussion activities provide ready-made tools for helping with critical reading and evaluation of content. The guides and activities deal with one or more of the following:

RECOGNIZING AUTHOR'S POINT OF VIEW

INTERPRETING EDITORIAL CARTOONS

VALUES IN CONFLICT

WHAT IS EDITORIAL BIAS?

WHAT IS SEX BIAS?

WHAT IS POLITICAL BIAS?

WHAT IS ETHNOCENTRIC BIAS?

WHAT IS RACE BIAS?

WHAT IS RELIGIOUS BIAS?

*From across **the political spectrum** varied sources are presented for research projects and classroom discussions. Diverse opinions in the series come from magazines, newspapers, syndicated columnists, books, political speeches, foreign nations, and position papers by corporations and nonprofit institutions.*

About the Publisher

The late Gary E. McCuen was an editor and publisher of anthologies for libraries and discussion materials for schools and colleges. His publications have specialized in social, moral and political conflict. They include books, pamphlets, cassettes, tabloids, filmstrips and simulation games, most of them created from his many years of experience in teaching and educational publishing.

READING **1**

A FRAMEWORK FOR UNDERSTANDING HUNGER

Amartya Sen

Amartya Sen is an economist who focuses on issues of poverty and famine. He was awarded the Nobel Prize for Economics in 1998.

■ POINTS TO CONSIDER

1. Define "the acquirement problem," "Malthusian pessimism" and "Malthusian optimism." How does each relate to a contemporary discussion of hunger?

2. How has population confused the hunger issue, according to Sen?

3. Summarize Sen's interpretation of Adam Smith's analysis of hunger. Describe other interpretations of Smith's work.

4. Discuss Sen's view on public intervention in the case of famine.

5. Evaluate the author's contention that the "food problem" should be seen in wider terms. Describe these broad terms.

© 1995 The United Nations. Reprinted from **The Political Economy of Hunger: Selected Essays** edited by Jean Dréze, Amartya Sen and Athar Hussain (1995) by permission of Oxford University Press.

Diverse policy instruments relate closely to "food policy" in the wider sense, affecting nutrition, longevity, etc., going well beyond the production of food. The "food problem" should be seen in these wider terms, involving not only the production of food, but also the entitlements to food and to other nutrition-related variables such as health services.

...One common feature of a good deal of instant economics related to food and hunger is impatience with investigating the precise mechanisms for acquiring food that people have to use. People establish command over food in many different ways.... I shall call the problem of establishing command over commodities, in this case food, the "acquirement problem." It is easy to establish that the acquirement problem is really central to questions of hunger and starvation in the modern world.

ACQUIREMENT PROBLEM

The acquirement problem is often neglected not only by non-economists, but also by many economists, including some great ones. For example, Malthus in his famous *Essay on the Principle of Population as It Affects the Further Improvement of Society* (1798) leaves the acquirement problem largely unaddressed, though in his less-known pamphlet, *An Investigation of the Cause of the Present High Price of Provisions* (1800), which deals with more short-run questions, Malthus is in fact deeply concerned precisely with the nitty-gritty of this problem.[1] The result of this neglect in the former work is not without practical consequence, since the popularity of the Malthusian approach to population and food, and of the particular metric of food output per head extensively used in the *Essay on Population,* has tended to give that metric undue prominence in policy discussions across the world.

Malthusian pessimism, based on the expectation of falling food output per head, has not been vindicated by history. Oddly enough, what can be called "Malthusian optimism," i.e., not being worried about the food problem so long as food output grows as fast as — or faster than — population, has often contributed substantially to delaying policy response to growing hunger (against a background of stationary or rising food output per head). This is a serious problem in the case of intensification of regular but non-extreme hunger (without starvation deaths but causing greater proneness to morbidity and mortality), and it can be quite disastrous in the context of a famine that develops without a decline in food output per head, with the misguided focus leading to a hopelessly delayed response of public policy. While Malthus's own writings are by no means unique in focusing attention on the extremely misleading variable of food output per head, "Malthusian optimism," in general, has been indirectly involved in millions of deaths which have resulted from inaction and misdirection of public policy.[2] While fully acknowledging the great contribution that Malthus has made in highlighting the importance of population policy, this negative feature of his work, related to his own bit of instant economics, must also be recognized.

POPULATION

The neglect of the acquirement issue has far-reaching consequences. For many years rational discussion of the food problems of the modern world was distracted by undue concentration on the comparative trends of population growth and the expansion of food output, with shrill warnings of danger coming from very respectable quarters.[3] The fear of population outrunning food output on a global scale has certainly not been realized, and world food output per head has steadily risen.[4] This has, however, gone hand in hand with intensification of hunger in some parts of the world. In many — though not all — of the affected countries, food output per head has in fact fallen, and the anxiety about these countries has often been anchored to the statistics of food output per head, with Malthusian worries translated from the global to the regional or country level. But a causal analysis of the persistence and intensification of hunger and of the development of famines does, in fact, call for something more than attention being paid simply to the statistics of food output per head....

FAMINES AND ENTITLEMENTS

The entitlement of a person stands for the set of different alternative commodity bundles that the person can acquire through the use of the various legal channels of acquirement open to someone in his position. In a private ownership market economy, the entitlement set of a person is determined by his original bundle of ownership (what is called his "endowment") and the various alternative bundles he can acquire starting respectively from each initial endowment, through the use of trade and production....

A person has to starve if his entitlement set does not include any commodity bundle with enough food. A person is reduced to starvation if some change either in his endowment (e.g., alienation of land, or loss of labor power due to ill health), or in his exchange entitlement mapping (e.g., fall in wages, rise in food prices, loss of employment, drop in the price of the goods he produces and sells), makes it no longer possible for him to acquire any commodity bundle with enough food....

ADAM SMITH

The point is often made that Adam Smith was a great believer in the simple theory of food availability decline in explaining all famines, and that he would have thus had little patience for discussion of entitlements and their determinants. Indeed, it is true that in his often-quoted "Digression Concerning the Corn Trade and Corn Laws" in Book IV of *The Wealth of Nations,* Adam Smith did remark that "a dearth never has arisen from any combination among the inland dealers in corn, nor from any other cause but a real scarcity, occasioned sometimes, perhaps, and in some particular places, by the waste of war, but in by far the greatest number of cases, by the fault of the seasons."[5] However, in understanding the point that Adam Smith is making here, it is important to recognize that he is primarily denying that traders could cause famine through collusion, and he is disputing the view that famines often follow from artificial shortages created by traders, and asserting the importance of what he calls "a real scarcity."...

We have to look elsewhere in *The Wealth of Nations* to see how acutely concerned Adam Smith was with the acquirement problem in analyzing what he called "want, famine, and mortality." I quote Smith from the chapter called "Of the Wages of Labor" from Book I of *The Wealth of Nations. (see sidebar, p. 11):*

Here Adam Smith is focusing on the market-based entitlement of laborers, and its independence on employment and real wages, and explaining famine from that perspective. This should, of course, come as no surprise. In denying that artificial scarcity engineered by collusive traders can cause famine, Adam Smith was in no way closing the door to the economic analysis of various different real influences on the ability of different groups to command food in the market, in particular the values of wages and employment....

10

RELIEF, FOOD AND CASH

BUT IT WOULD BE OTHERWISE IN A COUNTRY WHERE THE FUNDS DESTINED FOR THE MAINTENANCE OF LABOR WERE SENSIBLY DECAYING. EVERY YEAR THE DEMAND FOR SERVANTS AND LABORERS WOULD, IN ALL THE DIFFERENT CLASSES OF EMPLOYMENT, BE LESS THAN IT HAD BEEN THE YEAR BEFORE. MANY WHO HAD BEEN BRED IN THE SUPERIOR CLASSES, NOT BEING ABLE TO FIND EMPLOYMENT IN THEIR OWN BUSINESS, WOULD BE GLAD TO SEEK IT IN THE LOWEST. THE LOWEST CLASS BEING NOT ONLY OVERSTOCKED WITH ITS OWN WORKMEN, BUT WITH THE OVER-FLOWINGS OF ALL THE OTHER CLASSES, THE COMPETITION FOR EMPLOYMENT WOULD BE SO GREAT IN IT, AS TO REDUCE THE WAGES OF LABOR TO THE MOST MISERABLE AND SCANTY SUBSISTENCE OF THE LABORER. MANY WOULD NOT BE ABLE TO FIND EMPLOYMENT EVEN UPON THESE HARD TERMS, BUT WOULD EITHER STARVE, OR BE DRIVEN TO SEEK A SUBSISTENCE EITHER BY BEGGING OR BY THE PERPETRATION PERHAPS OF THE GREATEST ENORMITIES. WANT, FAMINE, AND MORTALITY WOULD IMMEDIATELY PREVAIL IN THAT CLASS, AND FROM THENCE EXTEND THEMSELVES TO ALL THE SUPERIOR CLASSES.[6]

A person's ability to command food has two distinct elements, namely, his "pull" and the supplier's "response." In the price mechanism the two elements are integrally related to each other. But in terms of the logistics of providing the person with food, the two elements may, in some contexts, be usefully distinguishable. If a person has to starve because he has lost his employment and has no means of buying food, then that is a failure originating on the "pull" side. If, on the other hand, his ability to command food collapses because of absence of supply, or as a result of the cornering of the market by some manipulative traders, then this is a failure arising on the "response" side.

One way of understanding what Adam Smith was really asserting is to see his primary claim as being one about the nature of "response failure" in particular, saying nothing at all about "pull failure." His claim was that a response failure will only arise from what he called "a real scarcity," most likely due to natural causes, and not from manipulative actions of traders. He may or may not have been right in this claim, but it is important to note that in this there is no denial of the possibility of "pull failure." Indeed, as is shown by his own analysis of "want, famine, and mortality" arising from unemployment and falling wages, Smith did also outline the possibility of famine originating on the "pull" side. There is nothing particularly puzzling or internally inconsistent in Smith's various pronouncements on famine, if we distinguish between his treatment of pull and that of response. It is not the case, as is often asserted, that Adam Smith believed that hunger could not arise without a crop failure. Also he was not opposed to providing relief through the "Poor Laws" (though he did criticize the harshness of some of the requirements that were imposed on the beneficiaries under these laws).

MANIPULATING MARKETS?

Smith's point that response failure would not arise from collusive action of traders has a direct bearing on the appropriate form of famine relief. If his point is correct, then relief could just as easily be provided by giving the deprived additional income and leaving it to the traders to respond to the new pull through moving food to the cash recipients. It is arguable that Smith did underestimate the extent to which traders can and do, in fact, manipulate markets, but at the same time the merits of cash relief do need serious examination in the context of assessing policy options.

Cash relief may not, of course, be quick enough in getting food to the starving in a situation of severe famine. Directly moving food to the starving may be the only immediate option in some situations of acute famine. There is also the merit of direct food distribution that it tends to have, it appears, a very immediate impact on nutrition, even in non-famine, normal situations, and it seems to do better in this respect than relief through income supplementation. These are points in favor of direct relief through food distribution. There is the further point that cash relief is arguably more prone to corruption, and that the visibility of direct food distribution does provide a better check. And the point about the possibility of manipulative actions of traders cannot, also, by any means be simply dismissed. These are serious points in favor of direct food distribution. But cash relief does have many merits as well....

As was observed in the Wollo famine in 1973 and the Bangladesh famine of 1984, and most spectacularly in the Irish famines of the 1840s, food often does move *out of* the famine-stricken regions to elsewhere. This tends to happen especially in some cases of slump famine, in which the famine area is short of effective demand. Since such "food countermovement" tends to reflect the balance of pulls of different regions, it may be preventable by distributing cash quickly enough in the famine-affected region....

If his analysis is correct — and the honors here are probably rather divided — the real Smithian issue in a situation of famine is not "intervention versus non-intervention," but "cash relief versus direct food relief." The force of the arguments on Smith's side cannot be readily dismissed, and the experience of mismanagement of famine relief in many countries has done nothing to reduce the aptness of his question....

MALTHUSIAN OPTIMISM AND INACTION

It has sometimes been argued that if a famine is not caused by a decline in food availability, then there cannot be a case for food imports in dealing with the famine.[7] This is, of course, a *non sequitur,* and a particularly dangerous piece of nonsense. Consider a case in which some people have been reduced to starvation not because of a decline in total supply of food, but because they have fallen behind in the competitive demand for food in a boom famine (as happened, for example, to rural laborers in the Bengal famine of 1943). The fact is that the prices are too high for these victim groups to acquire enough food. Adding to the food supply will typically reduce prices and help these deprived groups to acquire food. The fact that the original rise in prices did not result from a fall in availability but from an increase in total demand does not make any difference to the argument....

So far in this essay my concentration on policy matters has been largely on what may be called short-run issues, including the anticipation and relief of famines. But it should be clear from the preceding analysis, with its focus on acquirement and entitlements, that long-run policies have to be geared to enhancing, securing, and guaranteeing entitlements, rather than to some simple formula like expanding food output.

I have discussed elsewhere the positive achievements of public food distribution policies in Sri Lanka and China, and also in Kerala in India, along with policies of public health and elementary education.[8]

ENTITLEMENTS AND PUBLIC DISTRIBUTION

The role of Sri Lanka's extensive "social welfare programs" in achieving high living standards has been the subject of some controversy recently. It is, of course, impossible to deny that judged in terms of such indicators of living standard as life expectancy, Sri Lanka's overall achievement is high (its life expectancy of 69 years is higher than that of any other developing country — even those with many times the gross national product

MALTHUS, FOOD AND POPULATION

...Taking the population of the world at any number, a thousand millions, for instance, the human species would increase in the ratio of — 1, 2, 4, 8, 16, 32, 64, 128, 256, 512, and so on, and subsistence as — 1, 2, 3, 4, 5, 6, 7, 8, 9, 10, and so on. In two centuries and a quarter, the population would be to the means of subsistence as 512 to 10: in three centuries as 4096 to 13, and in two thousand years the difference would be almost incalculable, though the produce in that time would have increased to an immense extent....

On Population: Thomas Robert Malthus, Gertrude Himmelfarb, ed., New York: Random House, 1960.

(GNP) per head of Sri Lanka). But by looking not at the levels of living but at their rate of expansion over a selected period, to wit 1960–78, it has been argued by Surjit Bhalla and others that Sri Lanka has performed only "in an average manner." Armed with these findings (based on international comparisons of expansion of longevity, etc., over 1960–78), the positive role of Sri Lanka's wide-based welfare programs has been firmly disputed (asking, on the contrary, the general question: "when does a commitment to equity become excessive?").[9]

The basis of this disputation, however, is extremely weak. 1960–78 is a period in which Sri Lanka's social welfare programs themselves did not grow much, and indeed the percentage of GNP expended on such programs came down sharply from 11.8 in 1960–1 to 8.7 by 1977.[10] If the expansion of sowing is moderate, and so is the expansion of reaping, that can scarcely be seen as a sign of the ineffectiveness of sowing!

The really fast expansion of Sri Lanka's social welfare programs came much earlier, going back at least to the 1940s. Food distribution policies (e.g., free or subsidized rice for all, free school meals) were introduced in the early 1940s, and health intervention was also radically expanded (including taking on the dreaded malaria). Correspondingly, the death rate fell from 21.6 per thousand in 1945 to 12.6 in 1950, and to 8.6 by 1960 (all this happened before the oddly chosen period 1960–78 used in Bhalla's much-publicized "international comparisons" of expansions). There is nothing in the picture of "expansion" that would contradict the fact

14

of Sri Lanka's exceptional performance, if one does look at the right period, i.e., one in which its social welfare programs were, in fact, radically expanded, which happened well before 1960.[11]

INTERVENTION

The diverse policy instruments of public intervention used in Sri Lanka relate closely to "food policy" in the wider sense, affecting nutrition, longevity, etc., going well beyond the production of food. Similar relations can be found in the experience of effective public distribution programs in other regions, e.g., China and Kerala. It is right that the "food problem" should be seen in these wider terms, involving not only the production of food, but also the entitlements to food and to other nutrition-related variables such as health services....

NOTES FOR READING ONE

[1] Sen, A.K. *Poverty and Famines,* (Oxford: Oxford University Press, 1981).

[2] Sen, A.K. "The Food Problem: Theory and Policy," *Third World Quarterly,* vol. 4, 1982.

[3] The Club of Rome, despite its extremely distinguished leadership, had been responsible for some of the more lurid research reports of doom and decline.

[4] United Nations Food and Agriculture Organization, *The State of Food and Agriculture,* (Rome: UNFAO, 1985).

[5] Smith, Adam. "An Inquiry into the Nature and Causes of the Wealth of Nations," repr. in Adam Smith: *An Inquiry into the Nature and Causes of the Wealth of Nations,* R.H. Campbell and A.S. Skinner (eds.), (Oxford: Oxford University Press, 1976).

[6] Ibid.

[7] For a forceful presentation of this odd belief, see Bowbrick's paper (with a truly flattering title), "How Professor Sen's Theory Can Cause Famines," presented at the Agricultural Economics Society Conference, 1985, at the Annual Conference of the Development Studies Association.

[8] See Sen, A.K. "Public Action and the Quality of Life in Developing Countries," *Oxford Bulletin of Economics and Statistics,* vol. 43, 1981.

[9] See Bhalla, S. "Is Sri Lanka an Exception? A Comparative Study of Living Standards," in *Rural Poverty in South Asia,* T.N. Srinivasan and P.K. Bardham (eds.), (New York: Columbia University Press, 1988).

[10] These figures are given by Bhalla himself in a different context. He does not give the figure for 1978, but in his table the percentage had further dropped to 7.7 by 1980. Other sources confirm these overall declining trends during the 1960s and 1970s taken together.

[11] See Sen, A.K. "Sri Lanka's Achievements: How and When," in *Rural Poverty in South Asia,* T.N. Srinivasan and P.K. Bardham (eds.), (New York: Columbia University Press, 1988).

PART 1

HUNGRY FOR RELIEF: THE GLOBAL SOUTH, TRADE AND DEBT

READING

2

ORIGINS OF THE DEBT CRISIS

Jubilee 2000 United Kingdom

Jubilee 2000 is an international movement to cancel debt of impoverished countries.

■ POINTS TO CONSIDER

1. What events may have caused the U.S. to "spend more money than it earned" in the 1960s?

2. Discuss the reasons for Third World investment in the 1970s.

3. Why was the financial situation in Mexico in 1982 crucial?

4. Describe the international community's response to the debt crisis. How do the authors feel about Structural Adjustment Programs (SAPs)?

Excerpted from "How It All Began: Causes of the Debt Crisis," produced by **Jubilee 2000 Coalition** (United Kingdom), available at www.jubilee 2000uk.org/began.html. Reproduced by permission.

When Mexico defaulted on its debt repayments in 1982 the whole international credit system was threatened.

In the 1960s the U.S. Government had spent more money than it earned and to make up for this, decided to print more dollars. So the world's stocks of dollars fell in value.

This was bad news for the major oil-producing countries, whose oil was priced in dollars. The money they made from exports now bought less. So in 1973 they hiked their prices. They made huge sums of money and deposited it in Western banks.

Then the trouble really began. As interest rates plummeted, the banks were faced with an international financial crisis. They lent out the money fast, to stop the slide, and turned to the Third World, whose economies were doing well but who wanted money to maintain development and meet the rising costs of oil.

Banks lent lavishly and without much thought about how the money would be used or whether the recipients had the capacity to repay it. Third World governments, for their part, were pleased to take advantage of loans at very low interest rates — below the rate of inflation.

DEVELOPMENT

Some countries, like Mexico and Venezuela, took out loans to repay previous debts. But for others, this was the first time they had borrowed from commercial banks. Many intended to use the money to improve standards of living in their countries....

In the mid-1970s, Third World countries, encouraged by the West to grow cash crops, suddenly found that they weren't getting the prices they were used to for the raw materials they sold, like copper, coffee, tea, cotton, cocoa. Too many countries were producing the same crops, so prices fell.

Then interest rates began to rise, pushed further by an increase in U.S. interest rates. Meanwhile oil prices rose again. The trap was sprung — Third World countries were earning less than ever for their exports and paying more than ever on their loans and on what they needed to import. They had to borrow more money just to pay off the interest.

THE TRUE PRICE OF DEBT

...In Nicaragua, debt repayments exceed the total spending on social programs, yet three out of four people live below the poverty line and one out of four children under age five suffers from malnutrition. Honduras — where over half the population lives in abject poverty — spends more on debt service than on health and education combined....

"Debt Burden on Impoverished Countries," produced by **Jubilee 2000 Coalition** (United States), available at www.j2000usa.org/usa/edpac/debt.html.

THREAT OF DEFAULT

In 1982 Mexico told its creditors it could not repay its debts. The International Monetary Fund (IMF) and World Bank stepped in with new loans under strict conditions, to help pay the interest. The IMF is a Western-dominated creditor, which in effect acts as a Receiver but unlike a Receiver makes short-term loans to help countries pay off other loans.

This pattern was repeated over and over in the following years as other countries found themselves in similar situations to Mexico's. But their debts continue to rise, and new loans have been added to the burden.

Essentially, the poorest countries have become bankrupt.

When Mexico defaulted on its debt repayments in 1982 the whole international credit system was threatened. Mexico owed huge sums of money to banks in the U.S. and Europe, and they didn't want to lose it. So they clubbed together and got the support of the International Monetary Fund for a scheme to spread out or reschedule the debts.

Since then the IMF and the World Bank — the two main international financial institutions — have been involved in lending money and rescheduling debt in countries which, like Mexico, cannot pay the interest on their loans.

STRUCTURAL ADJUSTMENT

But their loans add to the debt burden and come with conditions. Governments have to agree to impose strict economic programs on their countries in order to reschedule their debts or borrow more money. These programs are known as Structural Adjustment Programs (SAPs). SAPs have particularly affected the countries of sub-Saharan Africa, whose economies are already the poorest in the world....

In order to obtain more foreign currency, governments implementing SAPs usually have to:

- spend less on health, education and social services — people pay for them or go without

- devalue the national currency, lowering export earnings and increasing import costs

- cut back on food subsidies — so prices of essentials can soar in a matter of days

- cut jobs and wages for workers in government industries and services

- encourage privatization of public industries, including sale to foreign investors

- take over small subsistence farms for large-scale export crop farming instead of staple foods....

READING

3

THE GOALS OF STRUCTURAL ADJUSTMENT

Staff of the International Monetary Fund

The International Monetary Fund (IMF) is a cooperative institution of 182 nations. Created during the post-WWII Bretton-Woods Conference, the IMF seeks to create a stable system of buying and selling currencies to smooth payments between countries.

■ **POINTS TO CONSIDER**

1. Discuss the reasons countries participated in structural adjustment regimes.

2. Summarize the goals of structural adjustment policies.

3. Describe the challenges to implementing structural adjustment policies.

4. In your estimation, how would these authors evaluate Sen's famine analysis from Reading One?

Excerpted from IMF Staff, "Initial Conditions and Setting for Adjustment," **The ESAF at Ten Years: Economic Adjustment and Reform in Low-Income Countries,** Washington, D.C.: The International Monetary Fund, 1997. Reprinted with permission.

It was apparent that fundamental economic reform was required to reverse trends and deliver a lasting improvement in growth and the external finances.

...Countries seeking support under the Structural Adjustment Facility (SAF) and Enhanced Structural Adjustment Facility (ESAF) had typically accumulated deep-seated economic problems over an extended period. Most came to the IMF in circumstances not of sudden macroeconomic or financial instability but rather of persistently weak growth, often chronically high inflation, and fragile external positions. Development strategies, based commonly on pervasive state intervention in the economy, public ownership, and protectionism, had left a dismal legacy. Distortions and rigidities were stifling entrepreneurship and promoting waste and corruption. They also aggravated the vulnerability of economies that were unusually prone to adverse economic shocks. In many countries, especially in Africa, these profound weaknesses had been masked during much of the 1970s by heavy foreign borrowing on the back of improving terms of trade. When commodity prices turned down sharply and interest rates rose in the early 1980s, both the debts and the policies they had financed became manifestly unsustainable.[1]

INITIAL CONDITIONS

The immediate need in most cases was to bring some order to countries' external cash flow positions, through a combination of debt relief or rescheduling and new resource flows. Even though many countries had already begun to adjust in the context of programs supported by stand-by arrangements, their external situations prior to SAF/ESAF-supported programs remained precarious: current account deficits (excluding official transfers) averaged 12 to 14 percent of gross domestic product (GDP), scheduled debt service was typically 35 to 40 percent of exports, and official reserves were uncomfortably low, given the volatility of these countries' foreign exchange earnings. External imbalances were particularly severe among future ESAF users in Central America and parts of Africa, much less so in Asia.

Net resource transfers did pick up sharply in the context of SAF/ESAF-supported programs. By this time, however, it was widely recognized that the debt crisis of the early 1980s was not a temporary problem of liquidity shortage — a matter of tiding over until the next upturn in commodity prices — but a true watershed.

Countries had become locked in a cycle of low saving, weak external positions, and low growth, with each element constraining the others. In the years leading up to their first SAF/ESAF arrangement (by and large, the early to mid-1980s), most were experiencing stagnant exports and declining living standards, with saving rates averaging only about eight percent GDP.

Certainly, the early 1980s were lean years for the developing world as a whole. But future SAF/ESAF users were on average falling further behind other developing countries in terms of *per capita* income during this period: their saving rates were half the average of other developing countries, and they had larger budget deficits, higher inflation, higher levels of external debt, more distorted exchange systems, faster population growth, and more adverse social indicators (such as education, health, and life expectancy). It was apparent that fundamental economic reform was required to reverse these trends and deliver a lasting improvement in growth and the external finances.

THE ADJUSTMENT STRATEGY

SAF/ESAF-supported adjustment programs varied widely in their emphasis and detail, in keeping with the differing circumstances of individual countries. But countries' common problems — and the universal underlying aim of achieving higher sustainable economic growth — resulted in reform strategies that shared certain core objectives.

First, to raise saving rates. The very low saving rates in ESAF countries were reflected in a combination of low investment ratios and high current account deficits. Since public dissaving was seen both as a root of this problem and as the most likely source of an early improvement in national saving rates, fiscal adjustment was at the heart of almost all SAF/ESAF-supported programs. Supporting policies, to bolster private saving, included financial sector reform and a shift from negative to positive real interest rates. The basic aim was to shift the macroeconomic balances underlying current account deficits in favor of greater investment.

Second, to secure macroeconomic stability. Although only nine of the 67 three-year SAF/ESAF arrangements covered by this review began with initial inflation rates in excess of 40 percent, most ESAF countries — with the exception of those in the CFA franc zone and some in Asia — had experienced volatile inflation for some years, with rates seldom falling into the single-digit range. This instability was viewed as disruptive, and a deterrent to investment. Programs aimed to reduce it by bringing inflation to low (single-digit) levels and by putting the government budget (a chronic source of financial instability) on a surer footing. Low inflation was also considered an important factor in improving conditions for the poorest sectors of the population.

Third, to liberalize and open economies to foreign trade. ESAF economies were generally inward-oriented with distorted internal relative prices. Producers faced substantial protection from external competition and disincentives against export activity. Programs sought to eliminate systemic anti-export bias through removal of exchange and trade restrictions (particularly quantitative import restrictions), exchange rate unification, tariff reform, liberalization of export price and marketing regimes, and public enterprise reform. In addition, in many cases, real devaluations of the domestic currency — secured by fiscal adjustment — aimed at enhancing the outward orientation of the economy.

Fourth, to reduce government intervention and promote well-functioning markets. The state needed to cease controlling prices, foreign exchange, and product marketing and by and large to withdraw from ownership and control of the means of production. Instead, its challenge was to establish a legal and institutional framework conducive to private business, where contracts could be enforced and property protected. The development of the financial sector was encouraged through a combination of financial and operational restructuring, privatization, and more effective supervision. Deregulation of pricing and marketing, public enterprise and banking system reform, and privatization were thus important structural components of SAF/ESAF-supported programs. The sequencing of reforms in these areas posed particularly difficult issues.

Fifth, to reorient government spending and restructure revenues. "Government," if represented by the share of its expenditure in GDP, was not unusually large in ESAF countries, but it was doing many of the wrong things. An excessive portion of government spending was devoted to subsidies for consumers and state-owned firms, wages for inefficient (or, in some cases, nonexistent) civil servants, ill-chosen capital projects, and the military. Programs aimed increasingly to reorient spending from areas with relatively low social and economic rates of return — unproductive spending

24

TABLE 1. ECONOMIC AND SOCIAL INDICATORS IN ESAF AND OTHER DEVELOPING COUNTRIES
(In percent a year, unless otherwise indicated)

	ESAF Countries		Non-ESAF Developing Countries[1]	
	1981-85	1991-95[2]	1981-85	1991-95[2]
Real per capita GDP growth	-1.1	0.0	0.3	1.0
Inflation[3]				
Mean	94.4	44.9	23.5	139.9
Median	11.7	11.6	9.1	10.3
Gross national savings (in percent of GDP)	8.0	9.9	18.6	17.4
Budget balance[4] (in percent of GDP)	-9.1	-5.6	-6.8	-4.8
Export volume growth	1.7	7.9	4.4	5.7
Debt-service ratio (actual) (in percent of exports of goods and nonfactor services)	27.9	25.7	18.8	15.7
External debt (face value in percent of GNP)	81.9	154.2	55.7	75.6
Gross reserves (in months of imports)	2.0	3.5	4.7	5.6
Premium in parallel market exchange rate				
Mean	230.5	18.3	49.0	201.2
Median	28.6	8.2	53.2	211.0
Population growth	2.8	2.5	2.4	2.2
Life expectancy (years at birth)	51.5	55.0	59.7	63.6
Infant mortality (per thousand live births)	111.9	87.5	71.8	52.7
Illiteracy (in percent of population age 15 or above)	54.8	47.3	32.2	23.0

Sources: Bredenkamp and Schadler (forthcoming); International Monetary Fund, *World Economic Outlook* and *International Financial Statistics*; and World Bank, *World Debt Tables and Social Indicators of Development.*

[1]Developing countries as defined in *World Economic Outlook,* excluding countries classified as "high income" by the World Bank and SAF/ESAF users.
[2]1991-94 for some variables.
[3]End of period when available, period average otherwise.
[4]Overall balance, including grants as revenue.

25

— to activities with high rates of return, such as primary education and basic health care. Revenue systems to finance these expenditures also needed to be rendered more efficient, through the simplification of tax and tariff structures, a move toward modern tax instruments such as the value-added tax (VAT), and more effective tax and customs administration.

Sixth, to mobilize external resources. A key part of the strategy under the ESAF was to support countries' reform efforts by temporarily easing the external financing constraint and to move them toward viability in part through reducing reliance on debt-creating inflows and, in some cases, debt burdens. Policies to this end included the clearance of payments arrears, agreements on debt reschedulings and debt relief, a shift to more concessional financing, and a rebuilding of official reserves.

THE SETTING FOR ADJUSTMENT

Reforms of this scope and magnitude would be challenging in the best of circumstances, and the environment within which policymakers had to implement ESAF-supported programs often complicated their task.

During the late 1980s and early 1990s, most countries had to contend with a sizable deterioration in their terms of trade as they embarked on their first SAF/ESAF-supported programs. The many countries for which tea, coffee, or cocoa was the principal export — almost one-third of all ESAF users — suffered from a 60 percent drop in world beverage prices between 1986 and 1992. Other nonfuel commodity prices — and, more generally, the growth of demand in ESAF users' export markets — weakened from 1988 through the industrial country recession of 1991–93.

Roughly one in four ESAF users also experienced severe civil strife or war during the late 1980s and early 1990s, in some cases associated with transition to more pluralistic political systems. In such circumstances, it was difficult to formulate policies, still less to sustain their implementation, and this was a factor contributing to the interruption or breakdown of a number of programs. In addition, many countries suffered from natural disasters during this time, including recurrent drought in sub-Saharan Africa and cyclones and flooding in Bangladesh and Nepal.

On the whole, market conditions improved for ESAF users after 1993. Nonfuel commodity prices (especially beverage prices) and the growth of global demand picked up markedly during 1994–95. At the same time, world energy prices remained subdued, at levels 20 to 30 percent below their peak in 1990. The prevalence of civil conflict also appeared to diminish in the mid-1990s, albeit with some striking exceptions (Burundi, Pakistan, Sierra Leone, and Sri Lanka). This generally more favorable climate seems to have continued in 1996, and is likely to have contributed to the widespread improvement in growth in ESAF countries during 1994–96.

CONCLUSION

ESAF countries suffered throughout the adjustment period, however, from restricted access to industrial country markets for key export products — particularly in agriculture, textiles, and clothing. Various international agreements defining market access, and granting preferences in some cases, contributed to segmenting markets and discouraging export diversification. Whether trade barriers were eased or intensified over time for ESAF users is difficult to determine: some preferential trading schemes have been broadened, with liberalizing effects; by contrast, some ESAF countries were adversely affected by increased protection in textiles and agriculture.

THE WALLS OF HUNGER: THE CONSEQUENCES OF STRUCTURAL ADJUSTMENT

Jack Nelson-Pallmeyer

Jack Nelson-Pallmeyer is a writer, professor and activist based in Minneapolis, Minnesota. He teaches Justice and Peace Studies at the University of Saint Thomas in Saint Paul and is the author of School of Assassins. *The following is excerpted from an article which appeared in* Connection to the Americas, *a monthly publication of the Resource Center of the Americas. The Center is a nonprofit watch-dog and advocacy organization focusing on Latin America.*

■ POINTS TO CONSIDER

1. Discuss some of the causes of hunger, according to Nelson-Pallmeyer. Which do the author believe to be the principal forces driving hunger?

2. Discuss the practical effects of structural adjustment regimes, according to the author.

3. Summarize what the author believes is the "intended byproduct of structural adjustment policies." What does the IMF intend? (See previous reading.)

Jack Nelson-Pallmeyer, "The Walls of Hunger," **Connection to the Americas** (a publication of the Resource Center of the Americas), February 1997. Reprinted by permission.

The deepening divide between rich and poor, between well-fed and hungry, is the fault line that will most likely determine the shape of our lives in the next century.

Around the year 2050, if present trends continue, one-half of all the world's people will live in absolute poverty and one of two U.S. citizens will be in prison. We may not want to imagine what life will be like in such a world, but present political, economic and military policies are taking us in this direction.

ABSOLUTE POVERTY

Environmentalist Alan Durning defines absolute poverty as "the lack of sufficient income in cash or kind to meet the most basic biological needs for food, clothing and shelter." For too many, the hungry future is now. Bread for the World reports that 1.3 billion people worldwide are "too poor to afford enough food to keep them fully productive." In the United States, one of four children is born into poverty.

Global statistics indicate that both the number and proportion of chronically hungry people declined from 1975 to 1990. This is, relatively speaking, good news. Hunger, however, remains a persistent, deadly reality. Nearly 20 percent of the "developing" world's population is undernourished and more than two billion people face vitamin and mineral deficiencies that pose serious health threats. And, despite the worldwide decline, the number of hungry people continues to climb in Africa, Latin America and the United States.

CAUSES OF HUNGER

The causes of hunger are numerous and complex. They include social-program cutbacks, a lack of living wages, tax policies, inequalities, and misuse of resources. In my view, however, the principle forces driving billions of people into hunger and destitution are the powerful actors reshaping the global economy. U.S. domestic and foreign policies in the 1980s and 1990s not only have aggravated today's problems of hunger and poverty across the Americas, they have paved the way for dramatic increases in hunger in the next century.

U.S. goals since the early 1980s, both domestic and international, have been to reduce the role of government in shaping national and international economies, to cut government social spending, to increase corporate power, and to redistribute wealth upward.

29

Austerity and structural adjustment programs have used Third World debt as leverage to force the changes.

From a business perspective, the results have been impressive. The 1980s marked the largest transfer of wealth in human history from the Third World to the First World, and the largest internal transfer of wealth from working-class U.S. citizens to the upper five percent of the population.

But from a human perspective, the "adjustments" have been devastating. "The 1980s was a lost decade for the South," Nicaraguan Jesuit economist Xavier Gorostiaga says. "There was a $500 billion net wealth transfer to the North…. The material basis for sustaining democratic expectations is just not there."

Neither is there a material basis for sustaining life itself, says former International Monetary Fund economist Davison Budhoo. "Between 1982 and 1990, the IMF's structural adjustment programs led directly to the deaths of some 70 million children under five years of age and to the destitution and impoverishment of several hundred million more. Not only children under five, but tens of millions of children above five, and an undetermined number of adults…have died or been put into destitution and absolute poverty by forced operation of the programs."

Significantly, U.S. tax and social policies in the 1980s resulted in a massive, upward redistribution of wealth in this country as well. During the decade, the income gains of the wealthiest one percent of our citizens exceeded the total incomes of 50 million U.S. workers. Not surprisingly, the number of hungry people in the United States has increased by 50 percent since 1985.

GLOBAL RULES

Hunger will intensify for many families as politicians scapegoat the poor and enact welfare "reforms," while diverting attention from those who have constructed the system that makes the United States the most unequal of all industrial societies. The gap between rich and poor continues to widen faster here than anywhere.

An intended byproduct of structural adjustment policies since the 1980s is that the terms of globalization have been set. Multinational companies go global as "a strategy for picking and choosing from a global menu," write Richard Barnet and John Cavanagh of the Institute for Policy Studies. "Vast areas of the world and the people who live there are written off."

COUNTING CALORIES

Some 64 million people were malnourished in Latin American and the Caribbean at the beginning of 1990. On average, they consumed 580 calories less each day than the 2,700 defined as sufficient. This crisis followed a decade in which calorie consumption dropped an average of .2 percent per year. In the 1960s and 1970s, in contrast, nearly all Latin American and Caribbean countries saw sustained increases in food supplies. The annual calorie-consumption increases averaged .7 percent.

On the whole, conditions have improved slightly since 1990, but serious shortages persist in countries representing about 16 percent of the region's population. In Haiti, for example, 40 percent of the people are undernourished today. And, in segments of all countries, including food exporters, poverty and hunger continue. Nine Latin American and Caribbean countries are expected to fall short of the 2,700-calorie level by the year 2010. They include Bolivia, El Salvador, Guatemala, Haiti, Honduras, Nicaragua, Panama, Peru and the Dominican Republic.

Here's how a few continents and countries compared in 1990 (Cuba and Mexico have lost ground since then) in average daily calorie consumption per person:

United States	3,600	Mexico	3,092
Canada	3,600	Africa	2,300
European Union	3,500	Peru	2,037
Cuba	3,131	Bolivia	2,056
Argentina	3,098	Haiti	2,051

United Nations Food and Agriculture Organization in Jack Nelson-Pallmeyer, "The Walls of Hunger," **Connection to the Americas,** February 1997.

Today you either play by predetermined rules or you don't play at all. As a consequence, many U.S. workers are competing with their global counterparts in a race toward lowest-common-denominator wages and benefits. Already, one in five full-time U.S. workers earns poverty-level wages.

Hunger and poverty are predictable byproducts of economic

globalization, a system that links opulence to destitution like Siamese twins. Economist Gorostiaga cites United Nations statistics showing that the world's 358 billionaires have a net worth greater than the combined annual incomes of 45 percent of humanity. Our world, he says, is a "champagne-glass civilization." The richest 20 percent of humanity hoards 83 percent of the world's wealth while the poorest 60 percent lives and dies on six percent of the wealth, he adds.

Globalization fills the champagne glass further for the wealthy few while defining a huge segment of humanity as disposable. "As economies are drawn closer, nations, cities and neighborhoods are being pulled apart," write Barnet and Cavanagh. "The process of global economic integration is stimulating political and social disintegration....A huge and increasing proportion of human beings is not needed to make goods or to provide services because too many people in the world are too poor to buy them.

DISPOSAL

The problem of the 21st century for people with economic and political power will be what to do with these billions of disposable people. A few years ago, I attended a meeting with wealthy Nicaraguan business leaders who openly articulated the usually hidden question that flows logically from the vast inequalities generated by globalization. "How," they asked, "do we get rid of the poor?"

To some, the answer is easy. In Brazil and elsewhere in Latin America, armed vigilante groups with ties to government security forces simply murder street children. In the United States, the nation with the world's highest *per capita* prison population, we build more prisons.

The deepening divide between rich and poor, between well-fed and hungry, is the fault line that will most likely determine the shape of our lives in the next century. Business-as-usual will mean death, destitution and environmental bankruptcy.

On the other hand, the future need not be a mere extension of the present. Inequalities, hunger and visions that fracture our communities also offer opportunities for new visions, policies and alliances. The rich-poor divide is morally repugnant, environmentally unsustainable and politically explosive. Hunger could be one of the concerns that leads to progressive alliances that hold the key to a better future.

READING

5

TRADE IS KEY TO FOOD SECURITY

United Nations Food and Agriculture Organization

*The United Nations Food and Agriculture Organization (UNFAO)
convened the World Food Summit (WFS) in Rome in November,
1996. The second of its kind, it assembled 1,200 international hunger
advocates.*

■ **POINTS TO CONSIDER**

1. According to UNFAO, what is the major cause of food insecurity?

2. Assess the statement that "increased food production must be
   undertaken."

3. Describe how increased global trade can increase food security.
   (You may also refer to Amartya Sen).

4. Summarize Commitment Four of the Rome Declaration.

Excerpted from "Rome Declaration on World Food Security," **Rome: United Nations
Food and Agriculture Organization,** 1996. Reprinted by permission.

Trade is a key element in achieving world food security.

...We consider it intolerable that more than 800 million people throughout the world, and particularly in developing countries, do not have enough food to meet their basic nutritional needs. This situation is unacceptable. Food supplies have increased substantially, but constraints on access to food and continuing inadequacy of household and national incomes to purchase food, instability of supply and demand, as well as natural and man-made disasters, prevent basic food needs from being fulfilled. The problems of hunger and food insecurity have global dimensions and are likely to persist, and even increase dramatically in some regions, unless urgent, determined and concerted action is taken, given the anticipated increase in the world's population and the stress on natural resources.

We reaffirm that a peaceful, stable and enabling political, social and economic environment is the essential foundation which will enable States to give adequate priority to food security and poverty eradication. Democracy, promotion and protection of all human rights and fundamental freedoms, including the right to development, and the full and equal participation of men and women are essential for achieving sustainable food security for all.

Poverty is a major cause of food insecurity and sustainable progress in poverty eradication is critical to improve access to food. Conflict, terrorism, corruption and environmental degradation also contribute significantly to food insecurity. Increased food production, including staple food, must be undertaken. This should happen within the framework of sustainable management of natural resources, elimination of unsustainable patterns of consumption and production, particularly in industrialized countries, and early stabilization of the world population. We acknowledge the fundamental contribution to food security by women, particularly in rural areas of developing countries, and the need to ensure equality between men and women. Revitalization of rural areas must also be a priority to enhance social stability and help redress the excessive rate of rural-urban migration confronting many countries....

34

COMMITMENT FOUR

We will strive to ensure that food, agricultural trade and overall trade policies are conducive to fostering food security for all through a fair and market-oriented world trade system.

THE BASIS FOR ACTION

Trade is a key element in achieving world food security. Trade generates effective utilization of resources and stimulates economic growth which is critical to improving food security. Trade allows food consumption to exceed food production, helps to reduce production and consumption fluctuations and relieves part of the burden of stock holding. It has a major bearing on access to food through its positive effect on economic growth, income and employment. Appropriate domestic economic and social policies will better ensure that all, including the poor, will benefit from economic growth. Appropriate trade policies promote the objectives of sustainable growth and food security. It is essential that all members of the World Trade Organization (WTO) respect and fulfill the totality of the undertakings of the Uruguay Round. For this purpose it will be necessary to refrain from unilateral measures not in accordance with WTO obligations.

The Uruguay Round Agreement established a new international trade framework that offers opportunity to developed and developing countries to benefit from appropriate trade policies and self-reliance strategies. The progressive implementation of the Uruguay Round as a whole will generate increasing opportunities for trade expansion and economic growth to the benefit of all participants. Therefore, adaptation to the provisions of the various agreements during the implementation period must be ensured. Some least-developed and net food-importing developing countries may experience short term negative effects in terms of the availability of adequate supplies of basic foodstuffs from external sources on reasonable terms and conditions, including short term difficulties in financing normal levels of commercial imports of basic foodstuffs. *The Decision on Measures Concerning the Possible Negative Effects of the Reform Program on Least-Developed and Net Food-Importing Developing Countries,* Marrakesh 1994, shall be fully implemented.

OBJECTIVES AND ACTIONS

Objective 4.1:

To meet the challenges of and utilize the opportunities arising from the international trade framework established in recent global and regional trade negotiations.

To this end, governments, in partnership with all actors of civil society, will, as appropriate:

(a) Endeavor to establish, especially in developing countries, well-functioning internal marketing and transportation systems to facilitate better links within and between domestic, regional and world markets, and diversify trade;

(b) Seek to ensure that national policies related to international and regional trade agreements do not have an adverse impact on women's new and traditional economic activities towards food security.

Members of the WTO will:

(c) Pursue the implementation of the Uruguay Round Agreement which will improve market opportunities for efficient food, agricultural, fisheries and forestry producers and processors, particularly those of developing countries.

The international community, in cooperation with governments and civil society, will, as appropriate:

(d) Continue to assist countries to adjust their institutions and standards both for internal and external trade to food safety and sanitary requirements;

(e) Give full consideration to promote financial and technical assistance to improve the agricultural productivity and infrastructure of developing countries, in order to optimize the opportunities arising from the international trade framework;

(f) Promote technical assistance and encourage technology transfer consistent with international trade rules, in particular to those developing countries needing it, to meet international standards, so that they are in a position to take advantage of the new market opportunities;

(g) Endeavor to ensure mutual supportiveness of trade and environment policies in support of sustainable food security, looking to the WTO to address the relationship between WTO provisions and trade measures for environment purposes, in conformity with the provisions of the Ministerial Decision on Trade and Environment in the Uruguay Round Agreement, and make every effort to ensure that environmental measures do not unfairly affect market access for developing countries' food and agricultural exports;

(h) Conduct international trade in fish and fishery products in a sustainable manner in accordance, as appropriate, with the principles, rights and obligations established in the WTO Agreement, the UN Agreement on Straddling Fish Stocks and Highly Migratory Fish Stocks, the Code of Conduct for Responsible Fisheries and other relevant international agreements.

Objective 4.2:

To meet essential food import needs in all countries, considering world price and supply fluctuations and taking especially into account food consumption levels of vulnerable groups in developing countries.

To this end, governments and the international community will, as appropriate:

(a) Recognizing the effects of world price fluctuations, examine WTO-compatible options and take any appropriate steps to safeguard the ability of importing developing countries, to purchase adequate supplies of basic foodstuffs from external sources on reasonable terms and conditions.

Food exporting countries should:

(b) Act as reliable sources of supplies to their trading partners and give due consideration to the food security of importing countries;

(c) Reduce subsidies on food exports in conformity with the Uruguay Round Agreement in the context of the ongoing process of reform in agriculture conducted in the WTO;

(d) Administer all export-related trade policies and programs responsibly, with a view to avoiding disruptions in world food and agriculture import and export markets, in order to improve the environment to enhance supplies, production and food security, especially in developing countries.

Members of the WTO will:

(e) Fully implement the Decision on Measures Concerning the Possible Negative Effects of the Reform Program on Least-Developed and Net Food-Importing Developing Countries through the WTO Committee on Agriculture and encourage international financial institutions, where appropriate, to help least-developed and net food-importing developing countries to meet short-term difficulties in financing essential food imports;

(f) Refrain from using export restrictions in accordance with Article 12 of the WTO Agreement on Agriculture.

International organizations, and particularly UNFAO, will:

(g) Continue to monitor closely and inform member nations of developments in world food prices and stocks.

Objective 4.3:

To support the continuation of the reform process in conformity with the Uruguay Round Agreement, particularly Article 20 of the Agreement on Agriculture.

To this end, governments will, as appropriate:

(a) Promote the national and regional food security policies and programs of developing countries particularly in regard to their staple food supplies;

(b) Support the continuation of the reform process in conformity with the Uruguay Round Agreement and ensure that developing countries are well informed and equal partners in the process, working for effective solutions that improve their access to markets and are conducive to the achievement of sustainable food security.

International organizations, including UNFAO, will, according to their respective mandates:

(c) Continue to assist developing countries in preparing for multilateral trade negotiations in agriculture, fisheries and forestry *inter alia* through studies, analysis and training.

THE TRADE MYTH AND FOOD SECURITY

Anuradha Mittal

Anuradha Mittal is the Policy Director at the Institute for Food and Development Policy or Food First. Food First is a nonprofit policy center based in San Francisco which highlights root causes and value-based solutions to hunger and poverty.

■ POINTS TO CONSIDER

1. Identify the three central characteristics of the new international food regime, according to Mittal.

2. Assess the statement "more trade equals higher national income and food security" from the author's point of view.

3. Explain the effects of trade on small and subsistence farmers, according to the reading.

4. According to the author, what is the "real" meaning of trade liberalization for the Third World?

Excerpted from Anuradha Mittal, **Freedom to Trade v. Freedom from Hunger: Food Security in the Age of Economic Globalization,** San Francisco: Institute for Food and Development Policy, 1997. Reprinted with permission

Transnational capital is playing a greater role in the world food provisioning system under the guise of free trade and unrestricted foreign capital flows.

The giant 1974 Rome Food Conference ambitiously declared its intention to wipe out starvation within a decade. Over a quarter century later, despite the technological leaps made in food production, the world is still characterized by over 800 million chronically undernourished people. November 1996 some 1,200 international community representatives of farmers, human rights and anti-hunger groups, women's organizations, environmentalist groups, etc., from over 80 countries again assembled in Rome at the Second World Food Summit (WFS) and Non-governmental Organizations (NGO) Forum, convened by the Food and Agriculture Organization of the United Nations, for the first such meeting since 1974. This time the bureaucrats and politicians gathered at the headquarters of the Food and Agriculture Organization (FAO) declared their intention to reduce by half the number of malnourished by the year 2015.

FREE MARKET IDEOLOGY

Much has changed in the intervening years. Today's lower expectations have been shaped by the ascendancy of a free market ideology that argues that the best way to fight global hunger is through deregulation, privatization and economic reforms calculated to encourage foreign investment. On the Summit's opening day, U.S. Secretary of Agriculture Dan Glickman told the world: "Domestic market reforms have unleashed the full potential of American agriculture. Our farmers now plant for world demand instead of for government programs."...

The new international food regime has three central characteristics that mark a break with the old system: First, national agricultural subsidies and protective tariffs are being removed in accordance with regional agreements like the North American Free Trade Agreement (NAFTA) and by the Uruguay Round of General Agreement on Tariffs and Trade (GATT). Secondly, transnational capital is playing a greater role in the world food provisioning system under the guise of free trade and unrestricted foreign capital flows. Finally, national economies in the Third World and the former Soviet bloc are being forcibly restructured under the auspices of structural adjustment programs. These

41

policy changes are contributing to a new export-oriented emphasis in agriculture and an unprecedented degree of economic inequality within and between countries and regions....

The FAO documents state the following:

_____

"TRADE HAS A MAJOR BEARING ON ACCESS TO FOOD *VIA* ITS POSITIVE EFFECT ON ECONOMIC GROWTH, INCOMES AND EMPLOYMENT...

TRADE IN FOOD WITHIN AND BETWEEN COUNTRIES IS VITAL TO WORLD FOOD SECURITY. WITHOUT TRADE, PEOPLE AND COUNTRIES WOULD HAVE TO RELY EXCLUSIVELY ON THEIR OWN PRODUCTION: AVERAGE INCOME WOULD BE FAR LOWER, THE CHOICE OF GOODS WOULD BE FAR LESS AND HUNGER WOULD INCREASE...

TRADE CONTRIBUTES TO INCOME GROWTH IN A NUMBER OF WAYS...IT IS ASSOCIATED WITH GREATER POSSIBILITIES FOR THE TRANSFER OF CAPITAL AND KNOW-HOW, PARTICULARLY THROUGH FOREIGN INVESTMENT...."

_____

While this may sound good in theory (see sidebar), a look at the real-life case of India provides some insights into this assumption. Trade liberalization has resulted in an India where the war on poverty did not fail — but rather has been called off. This is a key distinction. While agricultural exports in India have increased by more than 70% during the last five years of trade liberalization, and according to a recent report issued by Agricultural and Processed Food Products Export and Development Authority of India, its agricultural exports in basmati rice, wheat, and other cereals increased 35 percent from the year before, totaling $1.33 billion, food prices have increased by at least 63%, putting them beyond the reach of the poor. A survey by the National Institute of Nutrition shows that the *per capita* consumption of cereals has dropped by 14 grams per person per day since the late 1980s. The intake of lentils, the only protein source for many of the poor, dropped even more sharply....

TRICKLE-DOWN

The FAO documents argue that increased trade raises national incomes, and that this "trickles down" to each household. For example,

"Economic growth can increase individuals' command over resources and thus their access to food, and as incomes grow, the fraction spent on food declines and the chances of falling into food insecurity decrease."

In 1987-88 there were 361 million people in rural and urban India who were living in abject poverty, i.e., their income fell below the official poverty line. Today, data on consumer expenditure

42

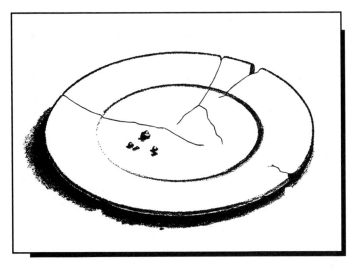

Illustration by Barrie Maguire. Reproduced by permission.

shows that the proportion of households below the official poverty line has increased, in both rural and urban areas.

According to an alternative economic survey conducted in 1994, the unionized sector in India was estimated at about 17% of the total workforce, which basically constitutes the middle class, estimated to be between 150-200 million. Yet with the industrial recession in the past three to four years, plant closures, non-payment of wages, temporary and permanent lay-offs have meant that the lower middle class has not been compensated for inflation. In fact the 200 million-strong Indian middle class market is being restructured. The lower end is being clipped off, while at the upper end incomes have increased remarkably. Surplus is being tranferred from the hungry population to the upwardly-mobile. The evidence for trickle-down is thus nonexistent.

HIGH INCOME EQUALS SECURITY

The third FAO assumption is that increasing household income will lead to greater food security, though even in the official documents some doubts were expressed:

> "...the impact [of trickle-down] may be more positive on the larger farmer producing cash crops and not necessarily on the small or subsistence farmers...."

43

The FAO staff further states:

This (see sidebar) has actually come true in India, in the rush to open up agriculture to big business. According to the Indian government's own estimates, some two million small and marginal farmers lose or get alienated from their land each year under current policies. Land reform has been removed from the agenda and we have a sure recipe for famine — putting the nation's food security in the hands of a few giant agribusinesses — while the poor are landless and unemployed. This will only get worse, as the new farm policy will further relax rural land-holding laws for businesses. The states of Karnataka and Maharashtra are already allowing entrepreneurs to buy large tracts of land.

For almost a decade the goal of major national and international food and farm policies has been to lower consumer food prices by increasing food imports. It is a well known fact that trade liberalization policies have kept farm prices in most countries at below-cost-of-production levels. This has put many farmers out of business, both in major exporting countries and in the importing countries. In the U.S., farmers were driven off their lands; the farming population fell from six million to two million in the Post-War period. Labor-saving technology drove small farmers out of business and led to the over-production which has created incentives to dump vast surpluses of under-priced grains in the Third World — in direct contradiction to GATT rules....

NEXT STEPS

We tend to lose sight of right and wrong when hunger is described with neutral terms like "food security," when the discussion should really be about values, that food is a basic human right. Reviewing the events of the past twenty years should leave no doubt in our minds. Since 1976, mass demonstrations in Peru in response to food price increases imposed by the International Monetary Fund, riots and austerity protests have

THE U.S., TRADE AND AGRICULTURE

Trade can take farm incomes and U.S. agriculture to new heights. But trade is not always predictable.

One of our most important trade policy efforts is the passage of "fast track" legislation. As the President has consistently stated, fast track is an important trade policy tool and the Clinton Administration is committed to securing fast track authority. At the same time, we are going to move ahead with a comprehensive trade agenda that seeks new opportunities for U.S. agriculture around the world.

Excerpted from the Statement of August Schumacher, Jr., before the Subcommittee on General Farm Commodities of the U.S. House of Representatives Committee on Agriculture, 25 June 1998.

taken place in dozens of countries as a result of similar policies....

The French Revolution was driven not only by ideas of political freedom, but also by the lack of bread in Paris. Food riots have occurred throughout the history of market societies, typically in conjunction with other non-violent forms of protest, whenever severe economic hardship, brought about by economic policies betrayed the moral basis of society and clashed with the basic human right to food.

For most of the Third World, trade liberalization really means neo-colonialism and a dominating and hegemonic world capitalist system, represented largely by the interests of the U.S. and a few other powers. The whole world was scandalized by the performance of the U.S. government at the World Food Summit. U.S. authorities refused to send any of their leaders to the Summit; and they rejected the final document which pledged governments around the world to reduce the number of hungry from 840 million today to 420 million by the year 2015. While the G77 countries, led by Cuba, called this "shameful," the U.S. delegation refused to support even that modest commitment....

The World Food Summit made it clear that the issue of food security is too important to be left to politicians, national governments or the marketplace. As the NGO community gathered in Rome and their statement made clear, the Summit's Action Plan with its focus on the Right to Food can only be realized with the concerted and single-minded cooperation of governments, organizations of civil society from the grassroots to the international level, and the multilateral agencies with a mandate in food and agriculture. More important, the transition to a restorative, sustaining democracy requires profound changes in our values and the way we understand human rights. The time has come to make the human right to food a reality. If we fail to exercise this right, we may lose our human rights altogether.

READING

7

DEBT RELIEF
IS HUNGER RELIEF

Jim McDonald

Jim McDonald is the International Policy Analyst for Bread for the World (BFW). BFW is a Christian organization in the U.S. which lobbies national decision makers on issues of hunger. Bread for the World Institute advocates for hungry people through research and education on policies related to hunger and development. Contact BFW at Bread for the World, National Office, 1100 Wayne Avenue, Suite 1000, Silver Spring, MD 20910, (800) 82 BREAD, www.bread.org.

■ POINTS TO CONSIDER

1. What is the "Jubilee Year" and from where does the idea originate?

2. Explain the need for Jubilee now, according to McDonald.

3. If the debt burden "is not so much the size of the debt," then why is debt relief an issue?

4. Describe the relationship, as the author views it, between debt and hunger.

Excerpted from Jim McDonald, "The Problem of Debt: We Are All Captives," **Bread,** May 1999.

The international debt owed by the poorest countries today simply cannot be paid without an unacceptable cost to poor and hungry people.

...The *Book of Leviticus* calls for a year of Jubilee every 50 years. People who have lost their land or liberty because of heavy debts are to be freed from this burden. They get their land, and their livelihood, back. Everyone gets a fresh start.

JUBILEE

The concept of Jubilee recognizes that, despite our best efforts, our social and economic relationships become distorted and unjust over time. Jubilee offers freedom from the destructive effects of political domination and economic injustice, and restores to all a sense of dignity and humanity.

Today, the world needs a year of Jubilee. Unpayable debt has a stranglehold on some of the most vulnerable people in the world's poorest nations. They are suffering because of bad choices made by others — past officials of their governments, and the countries and financial institutions who made the loans. Rich and poor, creditor and debtor — are all captive to a never ending cycle of unpayable debt that saps energy, resources, and ultimately hope.

The world's neediest countries repay staggering debts at the cost of increased hunger, disease and illiteracy. The world's richest countries, including the United States, and international financial institutions like the World Bank and the International Monetary Fund (IMF) try to collect unpayable debts at the unintentional cost of increasing environmental devastation and deepening economic and political crisis in the debtor countries. Jubilee offers release from the weight of debt obligations made morally unacceptable by the suffering they exact from poor people.

WHO REALLY PAYS FOR DEBT?

In 1996, the World Bank and the IMF identified 40 countries in Africa, Latin America and Asia as heavily indebted poor countries (HIPCs). These nations are home to nearly one-fifth of the world's population; 32 are located in sub-Saharan Africa. Their citizens suffer from malnutrition and unacceptable levels of illiteracy. At the same time, governments are unable to provide adequate health care services and access to affordable education. Although

Cartoon by Dan Wasserman. Reproduced by permission, **LA Times Syndicate.**

debt relief alone cannot solve the problems of hunger and poverty, debt relief would free financial and human resources needed to address those problems. Without debt relief, human development efforts are blocked.

The problem is not so much the size of the debt as the huge share of a country's income it gobbles up. In sub-Saharan Africa, governments owe foreign creditors an average of almost $400 for every man, woman and child — more than most Africans make in an entire year. Joao, a boy selling oranges in the interior of Mozambique, would need to sell 4,400 baskets of oranges to repay his portion of the debt. A teacher in Zambia would have to pay 14 months of her salary.

Debt repayments leave very little for much-needed poverty reduction programs and spending. In Tanzania, for every dollar spent on debt, only a quarter is spent on health care. The neglect is catastrophic. Life expectancy is only 50 years, and one child in six dies before age five.

In 1998, Mozambique's annual debt service obligation was more than half of its annual revenue. In a country still emerging from a sixteen-year civil war, more than half the population does not have access to safe drinking water, two-thirds of adults are illiterate, and most children do not go to primary school. The government's debt repayments, even though they fall well short of the amount due, are made at the price of investing in education, sanitation, immunization and other basic needs.

The debt burden also creates a double jeopardy for poor people. When highly indebted, poor countries go to the World Bank and the IMF for additional borrowing or to reschedule existing loans, they must also agree to a set of economic reforms known as structural adjustment programs, meant to help countries develop sound economies and bring what a country spends internationally into line with what it earns. The resulting dislocations and cutbacks in real wages and social services have been brutal for millions of poor people, however. Some countries have had to reintroduce school fees and charge for basic health services, which have put education and health care beyond the reach of many families.

AN UNPAYABLE BURDEN

Lending and borrowing among countries has long been part of the structure of the world economy. It often makes sense for developing countries to borrow foreign capital to fund roads, ports, agriculture, business, and improvements in health and education. The United States itself was a debtor nation for almost 150 years, from its origin until World War I. Today, as much as ever, the strength of the global economy relies on a solid system of international lending and borrowing. However, the international debt owed by the poorest countries today simply cannot be paid without an unacceptable cost to poor and hungry people.

The causes of the current debt crisis are complex. With few exceptions the poorest, most heavily indebted countries were former colonies. Most African countries did not win their independence until the 1960s or later. Just as Russia and the countries comprising the former Soviet Union are now having trouble restructuring their economies following the end of the Cold War, so too have these former colonies found it daunting to develop viable economies following independence.

DEBT'S LEGACY

In the early 1970s, Western banks were glutted with revenues from oil-producing countries as oil prices rose. Both the banks and rich governments encouraged developing countries to borrow heavily. Many developing countries, following the dominant

A STUDY IN DEBT: ZAMBIA

During a recent visit to Washington, D.C., five Zambian parliamentarians spoke passionately about the deprivation caused by their country's international debts.

Zambia owes more than $7.1 billion to donor countries and international financial institutions — almost $750 for every man, woman and child in Zambia. In this country where more than 70 percent of the population lives below the poverty line and one child in five dies before age five, debt is deeply felt.

The parliamentarians blamed Zambia's large overhang of debt for the lack of medicine in rural health centers, laboratories and libraries in schools, and recreational areas for children. In some areas, there are no schools or health facilities at all. Children who must travel long distances to attend school often end up dropping out, explained Charity Mwansa.

Such conditions lead to widespread discontent among voters, who subsequently do not vote, and to insecurity and an increased prospect of civil conflict, according to Dominic Musonda.

"I hope that some of the burden will be shifted from our shoulders" as a result of the Jubilee 2000 campaign, added Elizabeth Mulenga Chipampata.

Danielle Goldstone, "A Study in Debt: Zambia," **Bread,** May 1999.

development theories of that era, put great hope in grand government schemes and grabbed the opportunity such easy money presented. Loans were wasted on projects that did not work or were designed by aid agencies, involving huge contracts for foreign firms. Some borrowed money was pocketed by corrupt officials. Foreign loans also financed some countries' military buildup.

When global recession hit in the late 1970s, demand for exports dropped, and prices for agriculture and minerals plunged. Countries had to borrow more money, but interest rates had skyrocketed. Essentially, debtor countries were going bankrupt. But there is no legal proceeding for a nation to declare bankruptcy as individuals can. Over the last fifteen years, commercial banks and official creditors (i.e., governments and intergovernmental institutions) sought to address the problem by rescheduling loans and in some cases by providing limited debt relief.

Despite these efforts, the cumulative debt of many of the world's poorest countries continued to grow well beyond their ability to repay it. In 1986 the World Bank predicted that by 1995 sub-Saharan Africa would owe only $29 billion. In fact, by 1995, Africa owed seven times that much!

DEBT RELIEF IS HUNGER RELIEF

Nearly a decade ago, Bread for the World helped persuade the U.S. Congress to adopt legislation that canceled nearly $2.7 billion in poor country debt owed to the United States. In 1997, Bread for the World worked with the development group Oxfam America, the U.S. Catholic Conference and others to shape and support an international initiative to cancel some of the debt of highly indebted poor countries.

For the first time, the World Bank and the IMF agreed to write off some of the debt that low-income, highly indebted countries owe these institutions. This initiative, however, has not provided debt relief as deeply or quickly as is needed by poor countries. To strengthen this effort, Bread for the World now joins with Jubilee 2000, a global mobilization working to break the chains of debt that strangle the world's poorest countries....

READING

8

RELIEF AND AID: REWARDING SOUND ECONOMICS

The Economist

The Economist *is a weekly news journal based in London.*

■ **POINTS TO CONSIDER**

1. Summarize the most recent debt relief plan offered by the G8 in Cologne.

2. Identify some dangers which may result from the relief plan.

3. Discuss the legacy of aid, according to the authors.

4. According to the reading, what are the best predictors of economic success?

5. Describe the authors' design for foreign aid and debt relief. What solutions do they advocate in the case of nations led by corrupt leaders?

Excerpted from "How to Make Aid Work," **The Economist,** 26 June 1999. © 1999 The Economist Newspaper Group, Inc. Reprinted with permission. Further reproduction is prohibited. www.economist.com.

Aid should be directed only to countries with sound economic management.

"The poor always ye have with you," said Jesus, and 2,000 years of history have not proven him wrong. People who live permanently hungry, racked by parasites and forced to walk miles each day to fetch water, are more numerous now than ever before. Roughly 1.2 billion people — a fifth of the world's population — subsist on less than $1 a day. On June 18, 1999, at a summit in Cologne, the rich world's leaders came up with a plan to ease their plight.

COLOGNE INITIATIVE

Under the "Cologne Initiative" the G8 group of industrialized countries agreed to provide more debt relief, more quickly, to more poor countries. This, it is hoped, will release resources for health and education and generally make life in the Third World less miserable. Tony Blair, Britain's prime minister, spoke of "the biggest step forward in debt relief and help to the poorest countries that we have seen for many years." Perhaps. But that depends on how it is put into practice.

The Initiative is directed at the clumsily-named Heavily Indebted Poor Countries (HIPCs). The first comprehensive HIPC debt-relief plan dates from 1996. It aimed to reduce the debts of countries that maintained good economic policies to a "sustainable" level. This is calculated for most countries as a stock of debt (discounted to reflect its present value) equal to no more than 200 to 250% of annual exports. Alternatively, for extremely open economies, sustainability could be defined as a ratio of debt to government revenue of 280%.

Unfortunately, the original HIPC plan proved slow (only Uganda, Bolivia and Guyana have benefited so far) and stingy (in many cases the amount of debt service actually paid was likely barely to budge). Led by bishops, rock stars and charities, a loud campaign emerged to push for more and faster debt relief. The Scriptures call for forgiveness of debts every 50 years, some noted, reckoning that the next mass write-off was due in the year 2000.

The Cologne Initiative may fall short of millennial salvation but it is an improvement on its predecessor. The criteria for defining HIPCs have been broadened: a sustainable debt burden now implies a debt-to-export ratio of 150% or a debt-to-revenue ratio

54

Poor debtors
Net present value of debt as % of exports*

Country	Debt %	Total nominal debt 1997, $bn
Guinea-Bissau		0.9
Sao Tome and Principe		0.3
Burundi		1.1
Mozambique		6.0
Rwanda		1.1
Nicaragua		5.7
Zambia		6.8
Congo		12.3
Mauritania		2.5
Malawi		2.2
Sierra Leone		1.1
Ethiopia		10.1
Burkina Faso		1.3
Niger		1.6
Uganda		3.7

Sources: World Bank: IMF   *Pre-HIPC Initiative

"Poor Debtors," **The Economist,** 26 June 1999, p. 23.

of 250%, and it will be easier to qualify for the second.

Under the new plan 33 countries (with a total of 430 million inhabitants) are likely to be eligible for debt relief, compared with 26 under the original plan. And relief should arrive more quickly: the G8 have agreed to shorten the time a country must follow good policies before its debts are cut and to offer "cash-flow" relief in the meantime. Creditors also promised to include for the first time some $20 billion-worth of concessional loans in the debt calculation. When added to earlier pledges, the G8 claim, their efforts could reduce the stock of nominal HIPC debt by up to $70 billion: from some $130 billion today to as little as $60 billion. Viewed in present-value terms, the initiative itself offers debt reduction of $27.5 billion, which is more than double the $12.5 billion available before....

The danger is that the promised relief for HIPC debtors will either prove elusive or come at the expense of other aid and other recipients. Official aid flows have been broadly stagnant anyway throughout the 1990s — in part because aid has produced so few successes and so many mistakes. But there is hope in the fact that this initiative comes at a time when many donors — not least the World Bank — are rethinking their whole approach to aid. History offers one outstanding clue: if relief is not carefully aimed at countries with a genuine commitment to sound economic management, it will be wasted.

UNHELPFUL AID

Over the past 50 years rich nations have given one trillion dollars in aid to poor ones. This stupendous sum has failed spectacularly to improve the lot of its intended beneficiaries. Aid should have boosted recipient countries' growth rates and thereby helped millions to escape from poverty. Yet countless studies have failed to find a link between aid and faster economic growth. Poor countries that receive lots of aid do no better, on average, than those that receive very little.

Why should this be? In part, because economic growth has not always been donors' first priority. A sizeable chunk of Saudi Arabian aid, for example, aims to tackle spiritual rather than material needs by sending free *Korans* to infidels. During the Cold War, the Soviet Union propped up odious Communist despots while America bankrolled an equally unsavory bunch of anti-Communists. Keeping thugs like North Korea's Kim Il Sung and Liberia's Samuel Doe in power hardly improved the lives of their hapless subjects. Even today, strategic considerations often outweigh charitable or developmental ones. Israel gets the lion's share of American aid largely for historical reasons, and millions of American voters support it. Egypt gets the next biggest slice for recognizing Israel. Russia and Ukraine receive billions to ensure that they do not sell their surplus nuclear warheads.

Even where development has been the goal of aid, foul-ups have been frequent. Big donors like to finance big, conspicuous projects such as dams, and sometimes fail to notice the multitudes whose homes are flooded. Gifts from small donors are often strangely inappropriate: starving Somalis have received heartburn pills; Mozambican peasants have been sent high-heeled shoes. Poor research can render aid worthless: a fish farm was built for Mali in canals that were dry for half the year. The Turkana nomads of north-western Kenya, long pestered with ill-planned charitable projects, refer to foreign aid workers and their own government alike as *ngimoi:* "the enemy"....

GROWTH AND POVERTY

Gross domestic product (GDP) is not a foolproof measure of well-being. Wealth may be unevenly spread, so that a high average disguises widespread wretchedness. Nor does GDP take account of the hidden costs of pollution, for example. But when GDP grows, social indicators tend to improve with it....

Until recently, the fastest-growing emerging economies were clustered in East Asia whereas the disaster zones were disproportionately African. This led many to conclude that culture was the best predictor of economic success. Actually, sound policies and institutions, backed by liberal helpings of aid, are usually a better guide....

A recent study by the World Bank sorted 56 aid-receiving countries by the quality of their economic management. Those with good policies (low inflation, a budget surplus and openness to trade) and good institutions (little corruption, strong rule of law, effective bureaucracy) benefited from the aid they got. Those with poor policies and institutions did not. Badly run countries showed negligible or negative growth, and no amount of aid altered this. Well-run countries that received little aid grew steadily, with GDP per head increasing by 2.2% a year. Well-run countries with a lot of aid grew faster, at 3.7% per head a year.

Several things explain these differences. In countries with poor management, aid is sometimes stolen. Its effectiveness is often limited anyway by the fact that it tends to displace, rather than complement, private investment. In countries wih good management, aid "crowds in" private investment: if an economy is growing fast, the returns on road-building or setting up a new airline are likely to be high. A poorly managed, stagnant economy offers private investors fewer opportunities.

It seems clear that aid should be directed toward countries with good management and lots of poor citizens....

For countries with foolish leaders, a better approach than offering money is offering ideas. The architects of successful reforms in Indonesia in the 1970s, and in several Latin American countries in the 1980s and 1990s, were largely educated abroad, often at aid-givers' expense. The crash course in market economics given to top African National Congress members before they won South Africa's first all-race elections in 1994 helped turn them from

Marxists into fiscal conservatives. Ethiopia's new leaders took degrees in business administration in the mid-1990s.

RETHINKING AID

A condition of the G8's new debt-relief plan is that the cash it frees be spent on worthy things like education and health. The World Bank is well aware of the difficulties in ensuring that this actually happens but many donors are not. Aid-givers often finance specific projects, such as irrigation and the building of schools. Since the schools are usually built and the ditches dug, donors are satisfied that their money has served its intended purpose. But has it? Probably not.

Most evidence suggests that aid money is fungible — that is, that it goes into the pot of public funds and is spent on whatever the recipient wants to spend it on. If donors earmark money for education, it may cause the recipient government to spend more on education, or it may make available for something else the money that it would otherwise have spent on education....

Rich countries should be much more ruthless about how they allocate their largesse, whether earmarked or not. Emergency relief is one thing. But mainstream aid should be directed only to countries with sound economic management. The HIPC debt-relief plans, to their credit, do this. More donors should follow suit. Aid should also favor countries with large numbers of very poor citizens. India, Vietnam, Mozambique and Uganda, among others, meet both conditions. Many countries that receive substantial aid, such as Zimbabwe, Kenya and Russia, do not.

According to the World Bank, an extra $10 billion in aid could lift 25 million people a year out of poverty — so long as it went to poor countries that manage their economies well. The same sum spread across the current cast of aid recipients would lift only seven million out of destitution. In other words, aid could work if it were properly directed. And if taxpayers in rich countries saw their money actually doing some good, they might be happy to give more of it.

READING

9

PUNISH THE CORRUPT, NOT THE POOR

Robert Snyder

Robert Snyder is a Professor of Biology at Greenville College in Greenville, Illinois. He currently directs a program of international Christian agriculture ministries and formerly served as an agricultural missionary in Rwanda.

■ POINTS TO CONSIDER

1. Summarize the benefits of debt relief, according to Snyder.

2. Why is the author apprehensive about debt relief?

3. How should the international community treat heavily indebted poor countries in debt relief schemes?

4. In your own estimation, discuss the consequences of denying debt relief or foreign aid to corrupt leaders of heavily indebted poor countries.

Excerpted from Robert Snyder, "Proclaiming the Jubilee — for Whom?" **Christian Century,** 30 June 1999: 682-4. Copyright 1999 Christian Century Foundation. Reprinted by permission from the 30 June – 7 July 1999 issue of the **Christian Century.**

Quick fixes can sometimes become excuses for not dealing with the more painful fundamentals of international and national problems.

Jubilee 2000 is gaining momentum. Centers for the movement have arisen in more than 40 countries, and numerous churches and nongovernmental organizations have signed on to the campaign. The goals of this movement, which seems to have originated with the All Africa Conference of Churches and is now centered in the United Kingdom, are best summed up in the apostolic letter issued by Pope John Paul II in 1994. It states: "In the spirit of the *Book of Leviticus* (25:8-12), Christians will have to raise their voice on behalf of all the poor of the world, proposing the Jubilee as an appropriate time to give thought, among other things, to reducing substantially, if not canceling outright, the international debt which seriously threatens the future of many nations."

APPEALING IDEA

The idea is appealing. After all, there is no such thing as an international bankruptcy court which allows hopelessly indebted countries to declare themselves insolvent. Countries that have no hope of ever paying off their debt languish in a state of perpetual penury. The people of these countries barely eke out a living, while the banks owned by the wealthy prosper.

The world's financial institutions have recognized that something needs to be done to change this situation. The International Monetary Fund (IMF) recently started the Heavily Indebted Poor Country (HIPC) initiative, which singles out countries undergoing extreme financial stress. On the list are many African nations, including Rwanda, Burundi, Kenya and the Democratic Republic of Congo. Each country must pass a second screening to be eligible to receive some debt relief.

The Jubilee 2000 people claim that the relief proposed by the IMF is not enough. It does indeed seem to fall far short of what is needed. However, the concept proposed by Jubilee 2000 is riddled with pitfalls; to apply it universally would be naïve.

The economies of the heavily indebted countries would clearly benefit from debt relief. In countries with benevolent governments, the citizenry on the whole would gain. However, the socioeconomic structure of some of the heavily-indebted nations is such that, in the long term, debt relief might only aggravate the condition of the poor.

QUICK FIXES AND CORRUPTION

As a former agricultural missionary in east and central Africa, I've learned that quick fixes can sometimes become excuses for not dealing with the more painful fundamentals of international and national problems. A poorly executed act of sympathy can exacerbate the problem that it is meant to solve....

Though it is hard to prove, it is widely accepted that some African leaders promote ethnic violence during election times or when their power is challenged. The powerful are willing to injure and kill people so that they can continue to feed unhindered on the country's resources. Mobutu Sese Seko, the former president of Zaire (now the Democratic Republic of Congo), so ferociously plundered his country's resources that at his death his estimated worth stood at between $5 billion and $10 billion. His country's national debt was $14 billion.

Even some of the church leaders in such countries become involved in power games and ethnic divisiveness instead of serving as champions of justice. They, too, may have a vested interest in maintaining the *status quo*. We only need to consider our own history of race relations to understand how this can happen. Sometimes the flow of international charitable aid into the church attracts self-interested people into the institution; not all church leaders are oriented to serving the people. Many courageous men and women of the church have fought for justice, but many others have manipulated the system for their own gain.

CORRUPT POWER ELITE

Do we need to do something to help deeply indebted countries? Absolutely. Is the industrialized world partly responsible for their plight? Absolutely. Do we want to encourage corrupt leaders by giving them money that will enable them to pretend to be benevolent lovers of the people? Absolutely not. If we are going to forgive debt, let us not fool ourselves into thinking that we can outsmart the cunning men and women who are experienced at manipulating the international community for their own benefit. These leaders who are so good at sleight of hand will empty our pockets while they throw a few crumbs to the poor, and then laugh as their own bank accounts grow.

If a country is governed by a small, corrupt power elite and the national debt is really the debt of that elite, then let them face their people without foreign aid. The international community placed strong economic sanctions on the former white South African government. Even though those sanctions also impacted the poor, no one called for their discontinuation. Everyone agreed that ending the evil of *apartheid* required stern measures. Why can't we see that apartheid-like policies also exist in other countries? The world has shut its eyes to the racist policies of Rwanda and Burundi. Instead of imposing sanctions, we want to forgive their debts. When Kenya's leaders stir the country's racial tensions into riots, we look the other way and then talk about forgiving the government's debts....

FREEING THE OPPRESSED

Forgiving debts is a worthwhile enterprise, consistent with Biblical teachings. But the admonition to fight for the oppressed must equally be kept in mind. Forgiving a national debt and freeing the oppressed are not necessarily the same thing. In fact, they may be opposites. Let us proceed cautiously. We should not help any poor country that has a large, internally focused military or secret service. We must deal with more than the superficial issue of debt relief. The West must acknowledge its role in creating and supporting corrupt dictatorships. The economic powers need to help poor countries ruled by benevolent governments to get a sure footing in the international economic system.

Ultimately, we must realize that we in the West cannot "fix" the problems of the poor countries. The people themselves must rise up and say "no" to their corrupt power elites. They must say "no" to the petty corruption that occurs at every police station and customs office. They must say "no" to benefiting from the ill-gotten funds of family members with access to power. They must say "no" to preying on ethnic groups who are outside of the power clique. They must say "no" to corrupt spiritual leaders. Until this is done, debt relief will provide only a temporary respite, a time when leaders can rest more peacefully in their expensive villas. It will only camouflage the slow, under-the-surface boil in countries ruled by corrupt dictators and their minions....

RECOGNIZING AUTHOR'S POINT OF VIEW

This activity may be used as an individualized study guide for students in libraries and resource centers or as a discussion catalyst in small group and classroom discussions.

The capacity to recognize an author's point of view is an essential reading skill. Many readers do not make clear distinctions between descriptive articles that relate factual information and articles that express a point of view. Think about the readings in Part I. Are these readings essentially descriptive articles that relate factual information or articles that attempt to persuade through editorial commentary and analysis?

Guidelines

1. The following are possible descriptions of sources that appeared in Part I. Choose one of the following source descriptions that best defines each source.

Source Descriptions

a. Essentially an article that relates factual information

b. Essentially an article that expresses editorial points of view

c. Both of the above

d. Neither of the above

Source One

_____ "A Framework for Understanding Hunger" by Amartya Sen

Source Two

_____ "Origins of the Debt Crisis" by Jubilee
2000 United Kingdom

Source Three

_____ "The Goals of Structural Adjustment" by the
International Monetary Fund

Source Four

_____ "The Walls of Hunger" by Jack Nelson-Pallmeyer

Source Five

_____ "Trade Is Key to Food Security" by the United Nations
Food and Agriculture Organization

Source Six

_____ "The Trade Myth and Food Security" by Anuradha Mittal

Source Seven

_____ "Debt Relief Is Hunger Relief" by Jim McDonald

Source Eight

_____ "Relief and Aid: Rewarding Sound Economics" by
The Economist

Source Nine

_____ "Punish the Corrupt, Not the Poor" by Robert Snyder

2. Summarize the author's point of view in one to three sentences
   for each of the readings in Part I.

3. After careful consideration, pick out one reading that you think
   is the most reliable source. Be prepared to explain the reasons
   for your choice in a general class discussion.

PART 2

ABUNDANCE AND ANXIETY:
THE FIRST WORLD, HIGH-YIELD AGRICULTURE AND THE ENVIRONMENT

READING

10

GOOD SEEDS: THE GREEN REVOLUTION SAVED MILLIONS OF LIVES

Sharon Schmickle

Sharon Schmickle wrote the following as a staff writer for the Star Tribune *in Minneapolis.*

■ POINTS TO CONSIDER

1. Who is Norman Borlaug?

2. Discuss the meaning of the "green revolution."

3. Describe the origins of the green revolution.

4. Summarize the benefits of high-yield seed varieties.

5. In your estimation, what is the future of enhancing seed varieties?

Excerpted from Sharon Schmickle, "Hungry for a New Miracle," **Star Tribune,** 8 September 1991: 7A. Reprinted by permission, **Star Tribune,** Minneapolis.

The "green revolution," as it came to be called, saved tens of millions of people from starvation.

For three decades, breakthroughs in agriculture harnessed food prices in the United States and filled once-empty plates in many Third World nations.

But the technology that has averted a holocaust of hunger — doubling and tripling yields of some basic crops — cannot continue advancing at the pace that began in the years after World War II.

POTENTIAL FOR FAMINE

As the world's population grows by a projected one billion people in the 1990s, to 6.2 billion, agricultural experts are warning of a potential for famines. And they are renewing calls for birth control after a decade in which the U.S. government backed away from international population control efforts.

The "green revolution," as it came to be called, saved tens of millions of people from starvation. It propelled yields from Minnesota to Morocco. About 1.5 billion loaves of bread could have been baked from the yields that three new wheat varieties added to Minnesota's harvests in a ten-year period beginning in the mid-1970s, said Ronald Phillips, a University of Minnesota plant scientist.

Consumers have reaped many of the benefits, even if they didn't see the revolution unfold because their food gathering is limited to buying groceries. It has touched nearly every table in the United States.

In a fast-food meal, for example, the burger bun is made from wheat varieties that didn't exist in the 1930s; the meat and cheese, from animals fed new crop varieties; the fries and ketchup, from newfangled potatoes and tomatoes.

By producing food more efficiently, farmers have done their part to hold grocery bills in check. Grain prices have not kept pace with inflation or the costs of operating farms, so farmers depend on the ever-increasing yields to make up the difference.

But the green revolution's most vital results are taking place outside of the United States. Hunger was greatly reduced in many poor nations. India and Pakistan became self-sufficient in some

68

grains. China produced 435 million tons of grain [in 1990], up from 113 million tons in 1949....

CRITICS

Critics charge that the revolution simply postponed a crisis in the Third World by allowing more people to be born to eventual hunger, and that environmental and social costs are too high.

The revolution was based on "naïve" assumptions that hunger could be eliminated by growing more grain, said Daniel Janzen, a biologist from Minnesota who works in Costa Rica and is a professor at the University of Pennsylvania. Underlying political and economic causes of hunger weren't addressed, he said. "If all you do is make more food, you don't do anything," he said.

By most accounts, the revolution started in 1944 when scientist Norman Borlaug set out to help frustrated farmers find a variety of wheat that would grow on an inhospitable desert in northwestern Mexico.

Borlaug counters critics by saying it would have been immoral for developed nations to hoard agricultural technology they were creating.

"Starvation is not a very nice way to control population," he said. "We could still use that if you wanted, but if you start that approach, you'd better point a finger at medicine, too, because medicine moves into those countries stopping the epidemics that limit population."

STONE AGE TECHNOLOGY

Borlaug won the Nobel Peace Prize in 1970 for his work with wheat, but rejects credit for setting off the revolution. The technology really started when Stone Age hunter-gatherers began domesticating plants more than 10,000 years ago, he said.

The era of domesticated plants is a mere blink in human history, according to *Crops and Man,* published by the American Society of Agronomy. For 99 percent of the two million years of known human history, people didn't cultivate crops.

The founding farmers overruled nature's evolutionary judgment, hoarding seeds from the best plants and carting them around the globe. Through generations of such selection, the crops became distant genetic cousins of their wild ancestors.

But it was a hit-or-miss science. Famine was so common that members of most organized religions greeted each day with some variation on the Christian petition: "Give us this day our daily bread."

Not until the 1800s, after experiments with peas by the Austrian monk Gregor Johann Mendel, did anyone begin understanding the genetics behind the changes that farmers had wrought in crops over the centuries. And it wasn't until this century that plant breeding became the sophisticated science that Borlaug practiced in Mexico.

He drew on the sum of that technology to tackle problems with diseases and yields that were devastating Mexican wheat crops. Fertilizer didn't solve yield problems because it made the plants grow so tall they fell over. Mexico needed a new variety of wheat.

After more than a decade of crossing thousands of wheat varieties and weeding out the failures, Borlaug found the now-famous green revolution wheat: short, bushy plants that support abundant heads of grain, thrive on fertilizer and resist rust disease. The plants also were unusually flexible, and suitable for growing elsewhere.

SELF-SUFFICIENCY

By the late 1960s, Mexican varieties were helping countries such as India and Pakistan become self-sufficient in grain. At the same time, farmers reaped record harvests of rice that came from other breeding programs in Asia. Yields from corn hybrids, introduced on U.S. farms before World War II, were booming, too.

"The amount of rice and wheat grown in developing countries increased 75 percent between 1965 and 1980, while the area planted to the crops increased only 20 percent," said Edward C. Wolf, summarizing the revolution in a paper published by the Worldwatch Institute, a private study group in Washington, D.C. In all, he estimated that green revolution technology has added $56 billion to the value of the world's wheat and rice harvests.

The gains didn't come from plant genetics alone, but from the new varieties interacting with fertilizer and other technology. World fertilizer use increased fivefold between 1960 and 1988, according to United States Department of Agriculture (USDA) estimates. Farmers who could afford them also added irrigation systems and other chemicals.

From 1961 to 1985, the world's harvests increased by an average of 2.7 percent a year while the population grew by 1.9 percent a year....

ORGANIC COUP: A RENEWED FARMING VISION

Angel Mortel and Chad Ribordy

A young American married couple, Angel Mortel and Chad Ribordy are Maryknoll lay missionaries. After moving to Brazil in 1998, they recount their experiences in a column for the National Catholic Reporter.

■ POINTS TO CONSIDER

1. Describe the typical farming techniques in Brazil.

2. Why did Geraldo and Katia decide to farm? What "values" does organic farming espouse that appeal to growers and consumers?

3. Who are the main consumers of organic produce, like that which is grown by Geraldo and Katia?

4. Describe the pros and cons of alternative agriculture, in your estimation.

Angel Mortel and Chad Ribordy, "A Farm and a Vision of a Healthy Earth," **National Catholic Reporter,** 19 February 1999.

Although a day of working in the hot sun quickly dismisses all romantic notions of life in the country, there still remains a curious attraction.

There are no starving babies in this story. No descriptions of ill-functioning health, school or public services. No denunciations of corrupt government officials, nor of massive deforestation in the rain forest.

In short, none of the usual stories from Brazil that appear in the press. Although such stories are bountiful and deserve attention, it is also important to read about things that are working well here.

Enter Geraldo Magela Goncalves, Katia Mayumi Deyama and their two children, Taiyo and Yuri.

CHEMICAL-FREE

Geraldo, Katia and the children live outside a little town called Ibiuna in the interior of the state of São Paulo. They have a rather unusual occupation, for Brazil at any rate: They are organic farmers.

In a land in which much of the farming is large-scale and relies heavily on agrotoxins, Katia and Geraldo work their two hectares of land chemical-free. They grow cabbage, lettuce, broccoli, leeks, cilantro and a number of other vegetables. They have a couple dozen goats, a few chickens and two cows, whose primary purpose is to produce fertilizer for the farm.

They have two hired hands who help them work the garden: Adam, from the state of Minas Gerais and Andre, from the north-eastern state of Pernambuco. The latter, age 21, lives with his 15-year-old wife and their baby, Luis Carlos, in a simple little house right by the garden.

Katia and Geraldo met in 1990 at the University of São Paulo, one of Brazil's most prestigious universities. A degree from this school is a guaranteed ticket to the good life, a life accessible to only a select few. She studied history and he library science.

THE GOOD LIFE

How did such degrees lead to a life on the farm? Both look at each other and then respond, "Good question. You know we're not really quite sure." Geraldo grew up on a small farm in the

73

state of Minas Gerais. His parents encouraged him to study so that he could have a better life in the city.

Katia, on the other hand, is a "Paulistana" — born and raised in the city of São Paulo, home to nearly 18 million people. Both of them recalled that in their high school years they somehow came to value the country life and, more specifically, a life in the country without chemicals. It was Geraldo who began the farm in 1986, before he met Katia.

He bought a little plot of land in Ibiuna and with the help of his brother began to raise bees and goats, making the two-hour commute from the city on weekends. Taking advantage of his position as a librarian at the university, he was able to do a good deal of research on methods of organic farming.

By the time Katia and Geraldo married in 1994, the farm had grown and was demanding more and more time. Later that year, they took a giant leap of faith, gave up their life in the city, the promise of leading at least a middle-class lifestyle and moved onto their property in the country. At the time, Katia was six months pregnant with Taiyo. "A lot of the reason why we finally decided to move out here was for the sake of our child," they explained.

"Even though moving was a risk, we thought that city life, with all of its pollution and violence, is even riskier for the health of a child."

ALTERNATIVE MODEL

The two children, ages two and three, certainly seem at home on their farm. Katia and Geraldo have departed from the traditional farm model of the woman staying in the house and taking care of the children. For both philosophical reasons and the sheer demands of labor-intensive organic farming, they both work in the garden. Meanwhile, the children chase the chickens, play with the goats and pull up an occasional weed — and yes, vegetable — from the garden.

A city parent might look at the farm and see countless hazards for the kids. Yet Taiyo and Yuri move around the farm with a good deal of fearlessness and a certain amount of grace.

"We do not teach our kids to fear the animals or other creatures. With experience, they learn for themselves to have a healthy respect for the farm," explained Geraldo, pointing out a peck mark from Chico, the bully rooster, on Taiyo's back.

At current levels of operation and production, Geraldo and Katia will not get rich, nor will they become poor. The economic advantage of organic farming is that it is practically recession-proof here. Organic produce has a very specific market in Brazil — in the grocery stores of the rich. Those who can afford the produce will probably always have the money to buy it even when the country is having financial hard times.

LABOR INTENSIVE

The disadvantage of organic farming is that it is labor-intensive. To clear five rows of vegetables from weeds in Geraldo and Katia's garden takes an entire morning. In chemically controlled, weed-free gardens those hours are available for other tasks or for harvest. Yet Geraldo and Katia believe they have enough help.

Their problem right now is in method. "We are new at this and so make mistakes and lose a lot of time."

But for Katia and Geraldo, their farm is not just about business; it is about a vision. It is about a way of living and eating that is healthy for humans and healthy for the earth. They see that part of their work is raising awareness. For this reason, they participate in a local project called "Country-City-Life."

The organization seeks to connect folks from the city to folks in the country. The organization has a journal, a radio, a recycling center and a cooperative that buys products from small farmers. It then delivers and sells the goods in the city, giving back to the small farmers the maximum profit possible. Besides being the organization's treasurer, Geraldo also takes time to host guests of the organization who come to see his farm.

CURIOUS ATTRACTION

Although a day of working in the hot Brazilian sun quickly dismisses all romantic notions of life in the country, there still remains a curious attraction. Perhaps it is the simplicity. Perhaps it is the fresh air, blue sky, green trees. Perhaps it is the participation in meaningful work.

READING

12

THE BUSINESS OF FOOD

Kathryn Collmer

Kathryn Collmer was a freelance writer based in Minneapolis, Kansas, when she published the following in Sojourners. *She writes frequently on agriculture, environment and social justice issues.*

■ POINTS TO CONSIDER

1. What is the "worldwide phenomenon" the author writes of?

2. Before industrial agriculture, how did people get their food, according to the reading?

3. Describe the "transformation" of agriculture and its effect on the farm economy.

4. Define "vertical integration."

5. Discuss community-supported agriculture. (CSA).

Excerpted from Kathryn Collmer, "From Hand to Mouth," **Sojourners,** June 1993. Reprinted with permission from **Sojourners,** 2401 15th Street NW, Washington, D.C. 20009; (202) 328-8842/(800) 714-7474.

While every town's story is unique, each is merely a local variation on what has become a worldwide phenomenon — the industrialization of agriculture.

In every direction from Salina, Kansas, the proverbial amber waves of grain stretch to the horizon. A palpable excitement fills the air as farmers at the heart of the nation's breadbasket count down the days to harvest.

In Salina, a town of 42,000, many office workers save their two weeks annual vacation for June, so they can "go home" — which is wherever they have relatives who are still farming — and help bring in the harvest. People who work as secretaries or bank tellers by day will be driving combines and grain trucks long into the summer night. Nearly everyone you meet in Salina either grew up on a farm or has a close relative who did.

FOOD FROM SUPERMARKET

Yet even here, and even among farm families, most of the food on people's tables comes from the supermarket. And stores here are stocked with the same brands that fill grocery shelves all over the United States and, increasingly, around the world.

Gone is the Salina hatchery that for years supplied local families who raised chickens for eggs and meat. Gone, too, is the cheese plant that used to process milk from local dairies. Of the six flour mills that once hummed in this wheat capital, only one remains, and it is owned by a huge multinational corporation.

The story has been repeated in thousands of towns across America. In the smallest towns, where agriculture is the entire base of the local economy, the story ends in tragedy. As grain elevators, equipment dealerships, and other farm-related businesses fold, residents move away, the tax base dries up, schools close, more residents leave, churches empty out, and the town dies. While every town's story is unique, each is merely a local variation on what has become a worldwide phenomenon — the industrialization of agriculture.

It's a phenomenon of which we tend to be unaware — even though it touches most of our lives at least three times a day. Unless we make conscious efforts to support alternatives, we participate, with every meal we eat, in the global-industrial food system. This system has not only destroyed thousands of rural

Cartoon by Andrew Singer. Reproduced by permission.

communities but, through its reliance on pesticides, animal drugs, and chemical food additives, is gradually destroying our health. The system knows no national boundaries, nor does it respect cultural traditions, community bonds, human health, or the sacredness of life....

BODY AND SOUL

Just as food links the body and the soul, it also connects us as individuals with the rest of creation — not only with the soil and sunshine and water from which our food is formed, but with the many human beings whose work has brought it to our tables.

Until fairly recent times, most of the food people consumed was planted, harvested, and processed by themselves, their families, and neighbors. Even people living in large cities were supplied by the farmers in their own local region. The link between one's food and the rest of one's community was not theoretical but immediate and tangible.

Industrial agriculture has changed all that. Currently, each calorie of food you consume has traveled an average of 1,600 miles to reach you. That's largely because many functions that were once performed by farm families have been moved off the farm to wherever corporations can perform them most "efficiently."

Corporations achieve "efficiency" by using their vast stores of capital to build operations so huge — poultry houses containing up to 80,000 chickens apiece, for instance — that "economies of scale" come into play. This enables corporations to undercut the prices charged by smaller-scale farmers and processors, eventually driving them out of business.

However, corporate economies of scale are illusory; they only work because corporations are able to avoid paying the real social and environmental costs of their operations. For example, workers in chicken- and meat-processing plants have the highest rates of injury of any occupation, but wages and workers' compensation benefits in those industries are notoriously low. Corporate hog-farming operations, in which up to 30,000 sows are confined at one location, have polluted groundwater in at least 18 states, yet corporations have paid only piddling sums in fines.

Large companies are able to maximize profits by locating each segment of the food production process wherever costs can be minimized. Tyson Foods, for instance, raises and slaughters chickens in Arkansas, where environmental regulations are lax; processes the carcasses in Mexico, where wages are extremely low; then ships the final product to Japan for consumption.

Over the last 20 years, thousands of independent poultry growers in the United States have lost their poultry operations as a few dozen large corporations have taken over the nation's chicken production. Similar attrition has occurred in every sector of agriculture. As a result, less than four percent of the U.S. population lives on farms anymore, down from 30 percent in 1920. Like Native Americans, farmers have become a small, forgotten minority who are seeing their way of life destroyed. Forced to move to the cities, many find only unemployment and despair.

TRANSFORMATION

The transformation of agriculture has been fueled by a combination of government policy and consumer apathy. Tax loopholes and farm program incentives have favored large corporate agribusiness. Tyson Foods, for instance, with 1988 sales of more than $1.9 billion, was able to avoid paying any income taxes at all from 1981 to 1985.

Consumers, meanwhile, have focused on paying the lowest possible price for their food while ignoring the broader issues involved in how their food is produced. Yet the food supplied by corporate agribusiness is increasingly hazardous.

For example, approximately 5,000 deaths per year in the United States result from *salmonella,* a bacterium that spreads rapidly in the huge, crowded chicken factories where most of the nation's chicken and eggs are produced. Indeed, the U.S. Department of Agriculture estimates that 40 percent of the nation's chickens are infected with the deadly bacterium, which is transmitted to humans when chicken or eggs are not thoroughly cooked.

Adopting a meatless diet will not protect you from dangers in your food, either. In a report issued last year, the General Accounting Office concluded that up to one-third of the imported fruits and vegetables seized by the Customs Service because they contained pesticide residues that exceeded allowable U.S. levels ended up on grocery shelves anyway.

Obviously, we need greater accountability on the part of food corporations. That's difficult to achieve, however, when these corporations operate across national boundaries, beyond the control of any single government — and when the companies involved are so huge that their annual sales exceed the gross national product (GNP) of many countries. For instance, Philip Morris, the largest consumer-goods company in the world after having taken over Kraft and General Foods, had 1990 gross annual sales of $44 billion, a figure that exceeds the GNP of Israel, Portugal, or the Philippines.

VERTICAL INTEGRATION

Concentration of power is always frightening, but particularly so when it involves food. Today, half of our nation's food comes from the largest four percent of the farms, many of them run by large corporations that value profits above health and nutrition. Given that food, unlike cars, radios, or designer clothes, is a necessity that people cannot choose to forego, one wonders how long democracy will last as the food system becomes increasingly consolidated. As author Wendell Berry has written, "Political freedom means little within a totalitarian economy."

Indeed, less than 25 giant corporations now supply most of the items on American grocery shelves. That's not immediately obvious given the dizzying variety of food products on display....

Vertical integration has had a tremendous impact on family farmers. When farmers must both purchase their inputs from and sell their products to the same company, they are at the company's mercy, especially since companies typically charge high prices for inputs and pay low prices for crops. If the resulting squeeze is tight enough, farmers go bankrupt....

Another problem for farmers is that there are fewer and fewer buyers to choose from. Just six companies control 85 percent of the world's grain trade. Nearly 80 percent of the beef in the United States is slaughtered by only three meatpackers. With so few outlets for their livestock and crops, farmers are forced to accept however low a price the processors wish to pay.

Indeed, from a $2.59 box of breakfast cereal, the farmer who grew the grain in it typically receives about three cents. The remaining $2.56 covers processing, storage, transportation, packaging, and marketing gimmicks.

Surely there must be an alternative....

SEEKING AN ALTERNATIVE

The opportunity for city dwellers to get out to the countryside and dig their fingers into warm, rich soil is one of the chief attractions of what has come to be known as community-supported agriculture (CSA)....

In many cities around the country, that link is forged every week or even daily at farmers' markets. Unlike CSAs, farmers' markets are not a new idea. However, in recent years they've been gaining tremendously in popularity. Although they're less convenient than one-stop shopping at the supermarket, many consumers find that the extra trouble of making a trip across town is far outweighed by the benefits of buying fresh produce directly from the farmer. Some customers even develop ongoing relationships with particular growers.

Urban dwellers who would like to become growers themselves can join a community garden. Even in congested inner cities, community gardens are transforming vacant lots into verdant cornucopias. Individuals or families may plant whatever vegetables

ECOLOGICAL IRRESPONSIBILITY

...At present, it is virtually impossible for us to know the economic history or the ecological cost of the products we buy; the origins of the products are typically too distant and too scattered and the processes of trade, manufacture, transportation, and marketing too complicated. There are, moreover, too many good reasons for the industrial suppliers of these products not to want their histories to be known.

Where there is no reliable accounting and therefore no competent knowledge of the economic and ecological effects of our lives, we cannot live lives that are economically and ecologically responsible. This is the problem that has frustrated, and to a considerable extent undermined, the American conservation effort from the beginning. It is ultimately futile to plead and protest and lobby in favor of public ecological responsibility while, in virtually every act of our private lives, we endorse and support an economic system that is by intention, and perhaps by necessity, ecologically irresponsible....

Wendell Berry, "Back to the Land," **Amicus Journal,** Winter 1999.

---

they like in their own assigned plots, but all participants are asked to help with certain shared community tasks.

Of course, there will always be staples that even avid gardeners would find it difficult to grow in adequate quantities, such as wheat for flour. Rather than purchase these at the supermarket, more and more people are opting to join food cooperatives, which often specialize in organically grown or minimally processed foods. Co-op members typically make a commitment to volunteer a certain number of hours per week or month working at the co-op store in exchange for discounts on food.

Another popular arrangement is the "buying club," in which members pool their orders of such goods as beans, grains, dried fruits, and spices so that they can enjoy the price savings that come with ordering in bulk. When the shipment arrives, usually once a month, members gather to divide the bulk goods into the appropriate amounts for each household.

Since they weigh and package the goods themselves, members recapture the large portion of their food dollar that normally goes for packaging and advertising. These savings leave more money available to cover the often higher cost of organically grown foods. Thus, food dollars go toward real nutritional quality, rather than for a pretty (and often wasteful) package.

SECURITY

Most cooperatives and buying clubs obtain their goods from suppliers who share a commitment to supporting sustainable, chemical-free farming. Not only are such arrangements beneficial for consumers desiring safe, nutritious foods, but they are necessary to preserve family farming as a way of life. As corporate agribusiness destroys more and more farms, many farmers are deciding that their futures are more secure if they bypass the corporations and market their products through alternative channels such as cooperatives....

13

BAD SEEDS: DOUBTING THE FUTURE OF THE GREEN REVOLUTION

Peter Downs

Peter Downs is a freelance journalist based in St. Louis, Missouri.

■ POINTS TO CONSIDER

1. What is Monsanto?

2. How are seed companies employing technology to create new seeds? How are these seeds different from traditional hybrids? What are the author's concerns about this?

3. Discuss the problems with gene-altered seeds. Find examples of the success of gene-altered seeds. Use the print media or electronic resources.

4. Evaluate Monsanto's claim that it is a "bulwark against hunger." What is the author's view?

Excerpted from Peter Downs, "Bad Seed: Monsanto Sows Trouble on the Farm," **The Progressive,** February 1999. Reprinted by permission, Peter Downs.

If genetic engineering seed companies have their way, organic foods could disappear from America's menu.

Since 1996, the St. Louis-based agrichemical giant [Monsanto] has spent $8 billion buying up seed companies. Its purchases include Asgrow, the second largest soybean company in the United States, and Holden's Foundation Seeds, the source of the genetic material used in 35 percent of U.S. corn seed. It announced four more acquisitions in 1998....

If the Federal Trade Commission approves all of the acquisition deals, Monsanto will control an estimated 86 percent of the U.S. cotton seed market and nearly 50 percent of the corn and soybean seed markets. It will be the largest agrichemical company in the world, and the world's second largest seed producer after Pioneer. All of that market power will be concentrated in the hands of a company that has an unparalleled reputation for attacking competitors and silencing critics....

ORGANICS AND GENETIC ENGINEERING

If Monsanto and other genetic engineering seed companies have their way, organic foods could disappear from America's menu. "Organic standards do not allow genetically modified organisms," says Fred Kirschenmann, a large-scale organic grower in North Dakota. He says the genetic engineers are pushing farmers to use the genetically modified seeds that cost millions of dollars to develop. Kirschenmann's crops are from hybrids, which means he has to buy new seeds every year. He thinks that the current rate of buyouts and mergers will in five years seal off his access to high-quality seeds bred the traditional way, without genetic engineering.

Kirschenmann worries that seed standardization under large companies could mean no more organic vegetables. "It is clear to us that the Monsantos of the world will not have an interest in supplying a unique group of seeds for a small group of farmers," he says. Conventional farmers are also concerned that concentration in the seed industry will eliminate their choices.

But John Bobbe, economics adviser for the National Farmers Organization, says the chief concern about biotechnology is that it will turn farmers into contract workers on their own land....

RENTERS

Farmers "would be renters of germ plasm and seed, and contract for a bundle of services controlled by a megacomplex," agrees Michael Fly, director of the sustainable agriculture program for the Canada-based Rural Advancement Fund International.

"When you buy specialized seed from a company that also controls the market for the crop, you are in a totally contract situation. That is the end of the free market," says Kirschenmann. He says affected farmers may become totally dependent on their corporate employers.

Monsanto is the most hard-nosed of the seed developers. It doesn't just sell seed to farmers. It also sells them licenses to use the company's seed technology — licenses that forbid them from harvesting their own seed. Farmers were angry when they found that Monsanto licenses banned their traditional practice of saving seed. The company even required that they consent to on-site inspections to verify their compliance with the license agreement....

"Farmers are being turned into criminals, and rural communities are becoming corporate police states," says Hope Shand, research director for Rural Advancement Fund International. "We call it bioserfdom."

FLOURISHING?

The gene-tailored seeds are not always flourishing. Recently Monsanto introduced cotton varieties that did not perform well for some of the growers who tried them. In 1996, the insect-resistant Bollgard cotton seeds failed to stop bollworms in parts of Texas, Louisiana, Alabama, Florida, and Georgia. Monsanto had claimed the Bollgard variety was 95 percent resistant to bollworms. In 1997, growers in four Southern states who planted Monsanto's Roundup Ready glyphosate-resistant cotton complained of bolls prematurely falling off the plants. In both years, farmers had paid extra for the supposed super seed. Now the company faces class-action lawsuits from farmers seeking compensation for their losses.

Monsanto spokeswoman Kelly Marshall says the affected areas were relatively small and argues that the problems were the result of unusual weather. The extreme weather in 1996 caused an unusual bollworm infestation that simply overwhelmed the plants' defenses in some areas, she says, and a cold, wet spring (the second coldest on record) followed by a hot, dry summer affected plants in 1997. Could the problem be with genetic engineering? No, she says, "We didn't see it everywhere the seeds were used, and it is the same technology." But the Mississippi Seed Arbitration Council rejected Monsanto's weather defense and gave Mississippi farmers the green light to sue the company for damages.

In addition to its problems with cotton, Monsanto has had problems with canola and soybean seeds. In 1996, it had to recall 60,000 bags of canola seeds in Canada because they contained the wrong gene. In 1998, Missouri's soybean crop suffered severe losses from soil-borne fungus after farmers there planted glyphosate-resistant beans instead of disease-resistant varieties.

Jerry Flint, soybean technical manager at Monsanto, blames the problems on the weather, which he says has been more variable recently. That "makes it hard for farmers to predict what characteristics to select" in the seed they buy, he says.

But crop failure may be the least of the troubles.

CORPORATE CONTROLLED

Michael Fly suggests the seed standardization brought about by corporate-controlled genetic engineering could actually threaten the world's food supply. Restricting the source and diversity of seeds increases the risk of a cataclysmic failure of food crops due to climate changes or the emergence of a newly dangerous pest or disease. That threatens the quality of our air, water, and soil, says Fly.

Genetically engineered seeds may encourage overuse of herbicides, leading to the death of beneficial insects, and may even pass herbicide resistance onto weeds, critics add.

Marshall says genetic engineers are well aware of such dangers. It is foolish to think that Monsanto or any other company would do anything to harm agriculture or endanger food, "because then we wouldn't be in business," she says.

Fly doesn't buy that. "As with the nuclear industry and the pesticide treadmill, it is assumed that we as citizens will benefit from the positive side, and that we will pay for the downside," he says.

"I don't remember agreeing to that deal, and I'm sure a lot of other people don't remember doing so either."

HUNGER

Monsanto's latest public relations campaign paints the company as a bulwark against world hunger. At an event in St. Louis last July [1998] attended by former President Jimmy Carter, the company unveiled its new motto: "The seeds of the future are planted. Allow them to grow. Then let the harvest begin. Because securing food for our culture begins a better life for us all."

The Monsanto statement, which was to be run as an advertisement in Europe, suggested that health, safety, and environmental regulations will condemn millions to starvation. It said that failure to adopt agricultural genetic engineering is "a luxury our hungry world cannot afford."

But many nations are not willing to sign on. African delegates to a UN Food and Agriculture Conference in June [1998] issued a statement that genetic engineering was "neither safe, environmentally friendly, nor economically beneficial" to Africa. Citing the example of Monsanto's U.S. crop police, the delegates charged that Monsanto "stops farmers from...further developing their agricultural systems." By making African agriculture dependent on the purchase of imported seeds and chemicals, Monsanto will destroy agricultural systems and access to seeds and "thus undermine our capacity to feed ourselves," they said in their statement.

In November [1998,] the agriculture minister of India also rejected the company's claims. He asked Monsanto to leave India after learning that the company was testing genetically engineered crops there. That same month, Thailand banned genetically modified rice.

Neil Ritchert, from the Institute for Agriculture and Trade Policy in Minneapolis, calls Monsanto's talk about feeding the world "mythology." He says that Monsanto engineers seeds mainly for crops that serve as feed for industrial-farming applications, not food crops. With concentrated industrial agriculture, Ritchert argues, fewer people control access to food. The result is more hunger, not less.

Andrew Simms, a director of Christian Aid, a famine relief organization, says there is plenty of food to feed the world, but there is hunger because people can't get access to it.

CONTROL

Action for Solidarity, Equality, Environment, and Development, a coalition of youth groups in thirty European countries, kicked off a campaign against Monsanto and genetic engineering in November [1998,] called "Rounding Up Monsanto." It includes a *Monsanto Monitor* newsletter, leaflets, a directory of activists and actions to help local groups coordinate activities, and letter campaigns supporting the Brazilian ban on genetically engineered soybeans....

People still have time to stop the control of agriculture by corporate genetic engineers, says Fly, so "we aren't stuck with only one way to farm."

THE TRIUMPH OF HIGH-YIELD AGRICULTURE

Dennis T. Avery and Alex Avery

Dennis T. Avery is Director of the Center for Global Food Issues of the Hudson Institute. He was formerly a senior agricultural analyst of the U.S. Department of State. Alex Avery is a Research Associate at the Center for Global Food Issues.

■ POINTS TO CONSIDER

1. According to the authors, what is the greatest threat to wildlife? Why is it important to preserve wild lands?

2. In your estimation, how would the authors respond to the concerns of Reading Thirteen?

3. Examine the view of organic agriculture in this reading. Contrast this to the viewpoints in Readings Eleven and Twelve.

4. Define the family farm. What are the authors' views on trends in rural economic life? Do you agree with these?

5. What is the meaning of "sustainability?"

Excerpted with permission from Dennis T. Avery and Alex Avery, "Farming to Sustain the Environment," **Briefing Paper,** no. 190, May 1996, Hudson Institute.

We are not certain that high-yield agriculture can feed everyone and save all the wildlife habitat. We are certain that low-yield agriculture cannot.

Any discussion of agricultural sustainability must begin with the needs agriculture must meet. To be sustainable, an agriculture must first be sustaining. Agriculture's fundamental purpose is to supply virtually all our food and fiber. There is no visible, practicable substitute for *production agriculture* in this role.

We must also ascertain the scale of agriculture needed to meet current and future demand. Agriculture already uses approximately one-third of the earth's land area. Feeding and clothing a projected world peak population of ten billion will require a near tripling of the world's agricultural output....

SAVING WILDLIFE AND WILD LANDS

The leading threat to the world's wildlife is the potential loss of habitat to low-yield farming. Agriculture dominates the world's land use; already, one-third of the earth's land surface is in agriculture and one-third is in forest as "left over" from farming. Only by investing in sound, yield-increasing technology and practices can we prevent the loss of the remaining wild lands and creatures.

Wildlife and wild lands have great importance in our lives. The overwhelming reason for preserving them is to enhance our quality of life. Clearly, the wild places and creatures of this earth contribute enormously to the condition of humanity. A world without natural places for contemplation and perspective, without wild creatures to remind us of our place on this earth and to provide us with access to pure aesthetic beauty, would be sadly diminished. Because we have the *capability* to save the wild habitat and animals, we also have that *responsibility*. It would be arrogant and foolish to ignore it.

Under strict agricultural sustainability criteria, however, there are two other major reasons for preserving the world's remaining wildlife and habitats:

- First, forests and other nonagricultural areas are inextricably linked to the existence and maintenance of global climate patterns essential to current and future world food production.

92

- Second, these areas are urgently needed as a reservoir of genes and biodiversity for use in biotechnology. They are necessary to our ability to enhance and ensure the sustainability of our agricultural systems. A healthy, diverse, and dynamic pool of wild genes is essential to a truly sustainable agricultural system. Our crop and livestock breeders must keep pace with the increasing pressures on agricultural resources. As pests and disease organisms continue to adapt, farmers will need new crop and livestock genetics to minimize the damage they cause.

BIODIVERSITY

Wild genes are one of our biggest assets in meeting this challenge. They have been made directly useful by the new tools of genetic engineering, the most powerful crop- and livestock-improvement tools in history. Researchers are no longer confined to the genes from an organism's close relatives. The entire spectrum of genes from all organisms now has the potential to contribute to crop and livestock improvement and, therefore, has real technological value. Without a broad pool of natural genes to draw from, the benefits of these tools would be quite limited.

Fortunately, genetic engineering techniques will enhance our capacity to continue the rising yield and productivity trends which have protected wildlife habitats from conversion to agriculture throughout the past four decades.

THE ORGANIC DANGER

Relying on seemingly "benign" organic and other lower-yielding agricultural practices has been the sustainability solution offered by many, especially by environmental organizations. There is, however, considerable reason to question the sustainability of these systems on any large scale. If fears of pesticide and fertilizer impact push us toward lower-yielding alternatives, they will create a *far greater threat from the plow* to the ecosystems and wild creatures. Despite their advocates' claims of comparable yields, organic agriculture's yields per acre are sharply lower than mainstream yields when we include all the extra acres needed to sustain it: additional pasture acres for animal manure, cropland acres for "green manure," and cropland in nonyielding fallow periods.

Because these systems need more land to produce a given amount of food, adopting them globally would require farmers to convert large tracts of forests and other "suitable" wild lands to agriculture. Estimates of the land area necessary to meet demand in 2050 using strictly organic principles range as high as *25 to 35 million square miles* worldwide, rather than the current 5.8 million square miles now in crop production.[1]

Considering the possible changes to local, regional, and global climates and the inevitable decrease in biodiversity, the sustainability of these approaches is seriously in doubt. Even their rationality is highly questionable.

AN ENVIRONMENTAL PRIORITY

There is another reason related to wildlife and biodiversity for confining our agriculture to the land it now occupies. The best agricultural land also tends to have the least biodiversity. Michael Huston, an ecologist at the Oakridge National Laboratory and author of *Biological Diversity,* reports that, with few exceptions, biodiversity decreases as soil fertility increases.[2] The harsher lands have fewer resources, and competition among species is higher, which leads to increased diversity. America's Midwest and other areas with high soil fertility have relatively low numbers of exclusive plant species (one measure of biodiversity), with many states having none at all (Kansas, Iowa, Indiana, Ohio). States with larger areas of poor soil or low precipitation have the highest number of unique and exclusive plant species (California has 1,517; Texas, 379; and Florida, 385).

What this really means is that there is very little direct conflict between feeding the world and keeping the remaining wildlife as we triple world food output — *if* we continue to raise the yields per acre as we have for the past half-century, and thus confine our farming to the land currently in production.

Another factor often overlooked in discussions of how to preserve wildlife is the higher productivity of the best and best-serviced farmland (i.e., serviced by efficient infrastructure). The difference in yield between good, well-serviced farmland and marginal farmland can be tenfold or better. (Corn yields in West Africa currently average 0.7 tons per hectare, whereas the U.S. average is more than eight tons and rising, even though both sets of farmers have access to high-yielding hybrid seeds.) Bottom line:

it takes many low-yielding acres to match the output of one good acre....

WORLD FOOD DEMAND IN 2050

There are 5.8 billion people in the world right now. The *peak* world population will be nearly ten billion people, and it will be reached at or before the year 2050; the population will decline slowly thereafter.[3] The population peak is unlikely to rise to the 15 to 20 billion predicted by some doomsayers, mainly because of affluence and urbanization. Affluent city families tend to have fewer children than poor rural ones. Populations in most high-income countries average only 1.7 births per woman (BPW), well below the replacement level of 2.1 BPW. More importantly, the Third World has come three-quarters of the way to population stability since 1960, dropping from an average of 6.3 BPW to 3.2 BPW today.[4] Thus the global long-term trend is likely to be a slow population decline as most countries stabilize at about 1.7 BPW.

Even as affluence cuts birth rates, however, it is increasing the demand for *high-quality food* and, therefore, the burdens on the world's farming resources — land, water, feed supplies, inputs, etc. Trade is rapidly spreading affluence throughout the Third World, spurred by the First World's open trade commitments (such as General Agreement on Tariffs and Trade [GATT]) and special trade exemptions for poor countries (such as America's Generalized System of Preferences). Because of the increased emerging-country trade opportunities, Asia's gross domestic product (GDP) has grown by nearly ten percent per year for the last decade, and the trend seems to be spreading to Latin America, Eastern Europe, and other regions....

As their economies have boomed, Third World populations' personal incomes have increased, and a substantial part of the extra income has gone to improve diets. Diet improvement, especially including high-quality protein foods such as cooking oil, meat, and dairy products, is and will be a major factor in increasing demands on farm resources. These high-quality diets require more farm resources per calorie to produce than cereals. Likewise, a calorie of cooking oil takes twice as many resources to produce, and a calorie of meat requires three to five times as many farm resources....

We are *not* certain that high-yield agriculture can feed everyone and save all the wildlife habitat. We *are* certain that low-yield agriculture *cannot.*

The real myth endangering the world's environment — especially its wild lands — is that low-yield farming sustains the environment.

Because the world's agricultural output must nearly triple in the years ahead, no farming system can protect the environment and wildlife unless it achieves far higher yields than today's farms. If we fail to raise yields sufficiently to meet the increased demand, we will lose more wildlife habitat and wild species to plow....

THE CASE FOR PESTICIDES

The use of agricultural pesticides has long been one of the most hotly debated issues in environmental and agricultural circles. Opponents of pesticide use claim that pesticides are unsustainable because of their impact on the environment, wildlife, and human health, and because of the development of resistance in the pests. But a careful and thorough look at these issues fails to support their claims.

In fact, there is tremendous evidence that the judicious use of chemicals greatly *enhances* farming's sustainability.

Some antipesticide activists have asserted that agrochemicals have damaged the environment so severely as to decrease potential future production. This contention is refuted, however, by the ever-increasing yields on our fields. Every high-yield farm is a long-term testament to the viability and sustainability of today's agricultural practices, including pesticide and fertilizer use. The University of Illinois' Morrow Plots and the Rothamstead Plots in England, which go back many decades, along with other objective scientific studies of long-term farm productivity, support this assertion.[5]

The point is often raised that pest damage worldwide has increased dramatically despite pesticide use. But the real question is how high crop losses would have mounted *without* pesticides and how much extra land would have been needed to compensate for the losses.

(We must also note that organic producers also use large quantities of "organic" pesticides. Would pest damage decrease without organic pesticides? Are organic pesticides exempt from the accusations of environmental impact leveled against synthetic

96

THEOLOGICAL CONCEPTS

...The popular notion is that organic food contains no synthetic chemical additives. Defining just what this means in practice is hard enough. Are there any permissible measurable residues? How far down the production chain do the rules apply? If a field had synthetic pesticides applied to it in the past, how much time must pass before the produce grown on it can be called organic? What about the trace amounts of preservatives present in plastic packaging?...

Organic food may be technically difficult to define, but it isn't a technical concept at all; instead it has become a theological one. For many people, organic has come to mean a way of life — in the words of one group, a "holistic approach" involving "key concepts such as health of the agro-system and biodiversity."...

Sam Kazman, "The Mother of All Food Fights," **The Freeman,** November 1998.

pesticides?)

PESTS AND SUSTAINABILITY

Pests' resistance to pesticides is also raised in discussions of pesticides and sustainability. Pests will always adapt to overcome obstacles. Our only solution to pest adaptation is constant development of new pest-resistant crops, pesticides with new or altered modes of action, and prudent approaches to slowing the development of resistance in the pests. There is every reason to believe that we can continue to stay ahead of pest and disease organisms, especially in light of the potential of biotechnology. We cannot sit still on any broadly used pest controls, however, even natural ones such as the florally derived pyrethrin insecticides used by organic farmers.

The claims that agricultural pesticides wreak havoc on natural ecosystems are unrealistic for today's highly specific, low-volume, and short-lived pesticides. In addition, today's chemicals are applied very carefully, so that virtually all of their effects are confined to the fields where they are applied. For example, less than one percent of the herbicides applied in the U.S. leave the root zone of the fields.[6] The fields are far from being pristine natural environments; therefore, we can hardly burden our farmers with the task of creating ideal wildlife habitat within their fields while still demanding they produce high enough yields to protect the real wild lands from the plow....

UNDERSTANDING THE RISKS

Health risks from agrochemicals have been proven negligible. (Note: consumer health risks, or chronic low exposures, must be considered separately from *acute toxic exposures* to farmers and applicators from accidents and mishandling.) According to the American Council on Science and Health, recent increases in cancer in the U.S. are due almost entirely to tobacco, diet, alcohol, AIDS, and sun tanning. Better detection methods have also created the appearance of sudden increases in some cancers, such as breast and prostate cancer.

Two of the world's top cancer experts, Sir Richard Doll and Dr. Robert Peto of Oxford University, were retained by the U.S. Congress to assess U.S. environmental cancer risks. They concluded, "The occurrence of pesticides as dietary pollutants seems unimportant. There has been no increase in the incidence of liver tumors in developed countries since the long-lasting pesticides were introduced. Yet liver tumors are the most common form of cancer found in animal-based toxicological studies."[7] The American Council on Science and Health put it more bluntly: "'Chemicals' in food and the environment do not have significant impact on overall cancer risk in the U.S."[8]

John Graham, founding director of the Harvard Center for Risk Analysis, summed up the human health risk from pesticides when he noted that the U.S. regulatory safety standard for pesticide residues is no more than one additional theoretical cancer per million people, yet a person is five times more likely than that to be killed by a crashing airplane while standing on the ground![9]...

SMALL FAMILY FARM

What is a family farm? The family farm is a term subject to constant redefinition. The federal government defines a farm as "any agricultural enterprise which generates $1,000 or more from sales of agricultural commodities or food products." But technology has allowed one man to farm more and more acres. At the same time, the value of the off-farm jobs with which farming must compete has risen. As a result, average farm size has steadily increased. The average farm in the U.S. in 1950 was a little over 200 acres; today it is approaching 500 acres.[10] This is the average for all farms. If one were to survey only those farms where a majority of the household income is derived from the farm, the average size would be even greater. Accordingly, the number of farms has declined during this period, from 5.5 million in 1950 to 2.1 million today.[11]

The sustainability activists see these trends as a policy failure. It is unlikely, however, that national farm policy can preserve traditional and possibly inefficient farm structures or make people want to live in less hospitable areas. In fact, government programs and intervention have probably worsened the small-farm problem. Farm programs have *contributed* to the increase in farm size and destabilization of rural communities: price supports and payments have encouraged farmers to use debt leverage to buy out neighbors' farms. The federal subsidies let the high-tech farmer win twice — with greater sales and bigger payments. Without the certainty of federal price supports, fewer big farmers would have obtained the loans with which they bought out their smaller neighbors.

RURAL DEPOPULATION

Government farm programs have also played a major role in rural nonfarm depopulation, through land set-aside programs. One study estimates that land set-aside programs have cut the rural nonfarm population by 30 percent, because they reduce the amount of crops grown, transported, and processed; reduce machinery usage; and decrease demand for supporting businesses and services.[12]

Moreover, should preserving the *small* family farm even be our goal? The *family* farm is and continues to be the success model around the world. Virtually all of America's field crops and most of our meat come from family-owned and operated farms. Many people fear that as farm size increases and the number of farmers decreases, at some point the population density will fall below what is needed to support the nearby rural community. The real question for rural society, however, is not farm size but the overall economic viability of rural communities. What needs to be noted

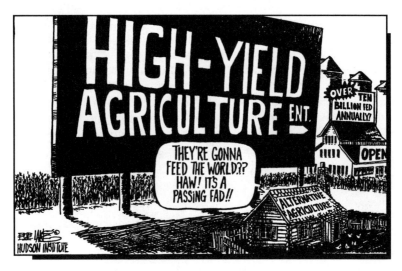

Cartoon by Bob Lang. Reprinted with permission, **Hudson Institute.**

is that *farming is not the biggest element of the economic base of most rural communities.* Three times as many basic industry jobs in rural counties are in manufacturing as in agriculture, forestry, and fisheries combined. Only 17 percent of the nation's counties are farming-dependent (deriving at least 20 percent of income from farming).[13]

Large farms produce the vast majority of agricultural products because larger farms are (1) bigger, (2) often more efficient in their use of off-farm inputs, and (3) often have higher yields per acre. By their very nature, small farms do not produce much income. It is still possible for people to live on eighty-acre subsistence farms in the Midwest, producing their own food, raising their own draft horses, and reading books from the public library by the light of kerosene lamps. Such farms would give us a higher rural population density, and they would certainly reinforce the old rural values of hard work and duty to the farm and family. Nonetheless, very few people choose to live that way, and those who do so contribute little to feeding and clothing the rest of us.

LARGE FARM

Indeed, the trend toward larger farms and the move to new strategies of production are realities that are difficult to overcome. Vertical integration may ultimately dominate in the hog and poultry industries because it makes them more cost-effective and competitive. It may also offer its labor force better incentives to stay in rural areas, by offering better financial opportunities and more comfortable lifestyles. (Many families are currently supporting an attractive rural lifestyle with contract poultry production.) It is impossible to de-invent these strategies. Making them more costly through farm policies directed at preserving the "small family farm" would hamper long-term U.S. competitiveness — and quite possibly make our rural *communities* less viable in the future. (Iowa has already lost some of its share of the hog market to other states because of constraints on farm size, structure, and odor imposed by its own rural communities.)…

SUSTAINABILITY AND OBJECTIVITY

As we examine the panoply of claims and countercharges about farming sustainability, it becomes abundantly clear that the opponents of modern, high-yield, chemically supported farming have made no attempt to examine objectively the sustainability of food production. They have started with an opposition to farm chemicals, thinly based claims that such chemicals harm humans and the environment, and an idealization of the rural communities of the past. They have gradually added other "sustainability" claims, and done so not on the basis of real-world food production but apparently on whether their assertions seemed likely to resonate with a public that they think has little understanding of agriculture.

The activists would like us to believe that they can deliver sustainability through organic and low-input sustainable agriculture. In reality, their "sustainability" would require us to shirk some of farming's major responsibilities: preventing hunger, producing sufficient high-quality protein, and protecting wildlife from the loss of habitat. Success in "environmental stewardship" is hardly success if it fails in any of these three duties.

Applying the term *sustainable* to alternative agriculture does not make it sustainable. Alternative agriculture may rely less on chemical inputs, but this is not a prerequisite for sustainability, and it could actually make farming less sustainable, by increasing land requirements. Today's modern, high-yield farming practices are the most sustainable we have ever had. They are continuing to change and improve in efficiency, safety, and sensitivity to the environment in direct proportion to our investments in agricultural research and technology.

CONCLUSION

The evidence of mainstream farming's gains in yield and sustainability reinforces the call for additional research investments to develop high-yield technologies further, to meet these goals and the increasing demands placed on agriculture, and to do so safely and without failing in our long-term responsibility to wildlife or the environment.

This is the single, major, inescapable conclusion of this study, which we believe is based on the real issues of agricultural sustainability, not on secondary social issues or unfounded fears.

NOTES FOR READING 14

[1] Dennis T. Avery, *Saving the Planet with Pesticides and Plastic* (Indianapolis: Hudson Institute, 1995).

[2] M. Huston, "Biological Diversity, Soils, and Economics," *Science* 262 (10 December, 1993): 1676-1680.

[3] Seckler and Cox, *Population Projections by the United Nations and the World Bank: Zero Growth in 40 Years*, Winrock International Institute for Agricultural Development, Center for Economic Policy Studies Discussion Paper No. 21, Arlington, VA, 1994.

[4] *World Development Reports,* World Bank, Oxford University Press, 1994.

[5] University of Illinois, *The Morrow Plots: A Century of Learning,* College of Agriculture Bulletin 775, Champaign, IL, 1984.

[6] Dr. Jerry Hatfield, Director, Soil Tilth Laboratory, Iowa State University, "Preserving Groundwater Quality," paper presented at the Hudson Institute conference "Saving the Planet with the 1995 Farm Bill," Washington, D.C., Feb. 7, 1995.

[7] Doll and Peto, *The Causes of Cancer* (New York: Oxford University Press, 1981).

[8] *Update: Is There a Cancer Epidemic in the United States?* (New York: American Council on Science and Health, Inc., 1995), 7.

[9] Testimony submitted to House Energy and Commerce Committee and Senate Labor and Human Resources Committee (Joint Hearing), "Safety of Pesticides in Food," *CIS* No. 94-H361-14, September 21, 1993, 153.

[10] Census of Agriculture.

[11] Ibid.

[12] Evert Van der Sluis and Willis L. Peterson, "Do Cropland Diversion Programs Harm Rural Communities?" *Minnesota Agricultural Economist* 677 (Summer 1994).

[13] Luther Tweeten, "Is It Time to Phase Out Commodity Programs?" Paper prepared for *Countdown to 1995: Perspectives for a New Farm Bill* (Columbus: Department of Agricultural Economics and Rural Sociology, The Ohio State University, 1994).

15

GLOBAL WARMING THREATENS THE FUTURE OF HIGH YIELDS

Robert T. Watson

Robert T. Watson was the Chair of the Intergovernmental Panel on Climate Change (IPCC). The IPCC is a United Nations-sponsored effort to synthesize the body of work concerning global warming and the effects of climate change.

■ POINTS TO CONSIDER

1. Discuss the relationship between climate change and food security.

2. Identify some of the effects of global warming on agriculture, according to the author.

3. Explain the possible effects of climate change on water. How does water relate to food security?

Excerpted from the testimony of Robert T. Watson before the Subcommittee on Energy and Environment of the U.S. House of Representatives Committee on Science, 6 November 1997.

Eight hundred million people are malnourished; as the world's population increases and incomes in some countries rise, food consumption is expected to double over the next three to four decades.

The overwhelming majority of scientific experts recognize that scientific uncertainties exist, but still believe that human-induced climate change is inevitable. The question is not whether climate will change in response to human activities, but rather *where* (regional patterns), *when* (the rate of change) and by *how much* (magnitude). It is also clear that climate change will adversely affect human health (particularly vector-borne diseases), ecological systems (particularly forests and coral reefs), and socio-economic sectors, including agriculture, forestry, fisheries, water resources, and human settlements, with developing countries being the most vulnerable.

FOOD SECURITY

Currently, 800 million people are malnourished; as the world's population increases and incomes in some countries rise, food consumption is expected to double over the next three to four decades. Studies show that on the whole, global agricultural production could be maintained relative to baseline production in the face of climate change under doubled carbon dioxide equilibrium conditions. However, crop yields and changes in productivity due to climate change will vary considerably across regions and among localities, thus changing the patterns of production. In general, productivity is projected to increase in middle to high latitudes, depending on crop type, growing season, changes in temperature regime, and seasonality of precipitation, whereas in the tropics and subtropics, where some crops are near their maximum temperature tolerance and where dryland, non-irrigated agriculture dominates, yields are likely to decrease, especially in Africa and Latin America, where decreases in overall agricultural productivity of 30% are projected under doubled carbon dioxide conditions. Therefore there may be increased risk of hunger in some locations in the tropics and subtropics where many of the world's poorest people live.

While the productivity of agriculture in North America is moderately to highly sensitive to climate change, the vulnerability is thought to be low at the continental scale, although sub-regional variation losses or gains are likely. For example, a warming of four to five degrees Centigrade is projected to lead to negative impacts in eastern, southeastern and corn belt regions, but to positive effects in northern plains and western regions. These model calculations have considered the positive effects of higher atmospheric levels of carbon dioxide, but have not fully considered the effects of potential dangers in climate variability, water availability, stresses from pests, diseases, and interactions with other existing stresses.

WATER RESOURCES

Currently 1.3 billion people do not have access to adequate supplies of safe water, and two billion people do not have access to adequate sanitation. Today, some nineteen countries, primarily in the Middle East and Africa, are classified as water-scarce or water-stressed. Even in the absence of climate change, this number is expected to double by 2025, in large part because of increases in demand from economic and population growth. Climate change will further exacerbate the frequency and magnitude of droughts in some places, in particular Africa where droughts are already a recurrent feature. Developing countries are highly vulnerable to climate change because many are located in arid and semi-arid areas.

SEA-LEVEL RISE

Sea-level rise can have negative impacts on tourism, freshwater supplies, fisheries, exposed infrastructure, agricultural and dry lands, and wetlands. It is currently estimated that about half of the world's population lives in coastal zones, although there is a large variation among countries. Changes in climate will affect coastal systems through sea-level rise and an increase in storm-surge hazards, and possible changes in the frequency and/or intensity of extreme events. Impacts may vary across regions, and societal costs will greatly depend upon the vulnerability of the coastal system and the economic situation of the country. Sea-level rise will increase the vulnerability of coastal populations to flooding. An average of about 46 million people per year currently experience flooding due to storm surges; a 50 cm sea-level rise would increase this number to about 92 million; a one-meter sea-level rise would increase this number to 118 million. The estimates will be substantially higher if one incorporates population growth projections. A number of studies have shown that small islands and deltaic areas are particularly vulnerable to a one-meter sea-level rise. In the absence of mitigation actions (e.g., building sea walls), land losses are projected to range from 1.0% for Egypt, 6% for Netherlands, 17.5% for Bangladesh, to about 80% of the Marshall Islands, displacing tens of millions of people, and in the case of low-lying small island states, the possible loss of whole cultures. Many nations face lost capital value in excess of 10% of Gross Domestic Product (GDP). While annual adaptation/protection costs for most of these nations are relatively modest (about 0.1% GDP), average annual costs to many small island states are much higher, several percent of GDP, assuming adaptation is possible.

SOCIAL COSTS OF CLIMATE CHANGE

Human health is sensitive to changes in climate because of changes in food security, water supply and quality, and the distribution of ecological systems. These impacts would be mostly adverse, and in many cases would cause some loss of life.

The range of estimates of economic damages caused by changes in climate are quite uncertain. Taking into account both market and non-market costs, IPCC reported a reduction in world GDP of 1.5-2.0% for a doubled carbon dioxide environment. This value was obtained by summing widely varying estimates of damages by sector, including socio-economic sectors (e.g., agriculture, forestry, fisheries), ecological systems, and human health.

CLIMATE CHANGE COULD HELP AGRICULTURE

Fred L. Smith

Fred L. Smith is President of the Competitive Enterprise Institute (CEI). CEI is a Washington, D.C.-based think tank which promotes market-based alternatives to political programs and regulations.

■ **POINTS TO CONSIDER**

1. Does the author believe in the certainty of global warming? Why or why not?

2. How does the author feel about efforts to curb global warming?

3. Describe the potential positive effects of global warming on agriculture.

Excerpted from the testimony of Fred L. Smith before the Subcommittee on Energy and Environment of the U.S. House of Representatives Committee on Science, 6 November 1997.

A warming pattern would likely lengthen growing seasons and, by reducing temperature variations over time, tend to reduce extreme weather events.

Most agree that the concentrations of carbon dioxide and other greenhouse gas levels in the atmosphere have increased significantly over the last century. (Water vapor which constitutes the vast bulk of all greenhouse gases at 90 plus percent is assumed to be constant, although little data exists on this topic.) Carbon dioxide has increased by 28 percent over this period, mostly in the last few decades; other greenhouse gas concentrations have increased as well. Concurrently, most scientists believe there has been a real, but slight (0.5 degrees C), increase in global temperature. However, human-induced increases in carbon dioxide levels cannot easily be linked to this temperature increase. Most of the observed warming (approximately 70 percent) occurred before 1940, while most of the greenhouse gas buildup occurred after 1940. Other trends, of course, may have obscured the warming impact, but the issue remains unsettled. Many temperature measurements are from urban areas that were once rural, biasing the temperature records upward. The less biased and more accurate source of temperature data, the satellite record, available since 1979, shows no temperature increase in recent years. Efforts to relate model predictions to empirical measurements continue but the situation remains unclear.

IS IT HAPPENING?

The computer models which suggest serious temperature changes are evolving rapidly, but still remain crude approximations of the complexities of the energy and material transfer systems that determine weather. Current computing capacity limits the "unit" of analysis to a very large volume of the atmosphere, rendering the models less useful for regional weather analysis. Moreover, the treatment of factors known to be key to climate remains weak. For example, the variability of solar radiation which some believe may well explain (without recourse to any greenhouse theory) most of the temperature variation of the last century is largely ignored. Water, which scientists increasingly recognize as the critical variable in the climate determination game, is handled unimaginatively. Dynamic interaction effects such as how warming might impact upon the amount, distribution and state (liquid, gaseous, solid) of water in the atmosphere are also addressed in rather rigid ways. Some have argued that the additional surface warming suggested by carbon dioxide increases would increase ground-level moisture levels and increase the strength of convection currents which move heat from the surface to the troposphere. The efficiency of out-radiation of heat there is influenced strongly by the dryness of the tropospheric air masses. If the overall impact of surface level warming is a less moist troposphere, then much of any initial greenhouse warming impact might be offset; if the effect is a moister upper atmosphere, then we might anticipate greater warming. Current models simulate these critical relations only imperfectly.

SHOULD WE WORRY?

Even if the scientific evidence were to suggest that man-induced global warming were a certainty, this would decide little. It is not temperature change *per se* that triggers the global warming concern, but rather views as to how such changes will affect our planet. Warmer weather will certainly have benefits — lower heating bills in the winter and greater agricultural productivity — but some argue it will also increase the frequency and/or severity of hurricanes or floods. Hurricane Andrew and the Mississippi-Missouri floods were disasters of unanticipated magnitude, and we should clearly be concerned if the frequency of such disasters is likely to increase. Here, however, the evidence remains so inconclusive that even the report of the UN Intergovernmental Panel on Climate Change stated, "Overall, there is no evidence that extreme weather events, or climate variability, has increased, in a global sense, through the 20th century, although data and analyses are poor and not comprehensive."

In fact, warmer weather may well be better weather. Evidence for this may be found in the terminology used by the English climatologist Hubert H. Lamb to label the two warmest periods of the last ten thousand years — the Climate Optimum around 5000 to 1000 B.C. and the Little Climate Optimum around 800 to 1200 A.D. Recent historical research by Dr. Thomas Gale Moore provides further evidence that warmer weather correlates well with better times. Such findings are compatible with current climate change theories, which suggest that if warming occurs, it will largely occur at night, in the winter, and at higher latitudes. Such a warming pattern would likely lengthen growing seasons and, by reducing temperature variations over time, tend to reduce extreme weather events. Furthermore, higher levels of carbon

WE SHOULDN'T FEAR GLOBAL WARMING

In many parts of the world, warmer weather should mean longer growing seasons. Should the world warm, the hotter climate would enhance evaporation from the seas, leading most probably to more precipitation worldwide. Moreover, the enrichment of the atmosphere with CO_2 would fertilize plants and make for more vigorous growth. Agricultural economists studying the relationship of temperatures and CO_2 to crop yields have found not only that a warmer climate would push up yields in Canada, Australia, Japan, northern Russia, Finland, and Iceland but also that the added boost from enriched CO_2 fertilization would enhance output by 17 percent....

Thomas Gale Moore, **Climate of Fear,** Washington, D.C.: Cato Institute, 1998.

dioxide increase plant growth and thus increase agricultural output. Thus, it is not clear that global warming is something that should be prevented, even if it were easy and cost little. Spending money to avoid better weather makes little sense.

In any event, the existing computer models (the basis of most global warming claims) suggest slow response rates to any changes in carbon dioxide levels, which implies that quick action now would have little impact on climate for many decades. One recent study suggested that delays on the order of a decade or so would have little impact on the temperatures that might be expected in the late 21st century. Since discontinuing any political program is extremely difficult, we should be very careful about locking ourselves into what may well be an unnecessary program. Science provides little support for the view that global warming is clearly upon us, that global warming will prove decisively harmful, or that urgent action is required.

WASTING AWAY: FACTORY FARMS AND POLLUTION

Tanya Tolchin

Tanya Tolchin works in the Sierra Club legislative office in Washington, D.C.

■ POINTS TO CONSIDER

1. Explain the source of the "millions of gallons" of waste, according to Tolchin.

2. What often happens to the waste?

3. Discuss the health concerns Tolchin addresses.

4. Describe the community concerns of the author.

Excerpted from Tanya Tolchin, "Wasting Away: Big Agribusiness Factory Farms Make a Big Mess," **Multinational Monitor,** June 1998. Reprinted by permission.

Big agribusiness companies deny responsibility for the environmental harms of factory farms.

...The sheer volume of animal waste produced on factory farms is astounding. The total amount of animal manure produced on U.S. factory farms each year, 2.7 trillion pounds, according to a report by the office of U.S. Senator Tom Harkin, D-Iowa, is the equivalent of an imaginary train of 6.7 million boxcars filled with manure circling the earth more than 12 times. The waste is often stored in open-air lagoons, or spread thickly onto fields, leaching and spilling directly into local streams, poisoning wells and destroying wildlife habitat. The problem of animal waste is far worse in concentrated animal feeding operations than on family farms simply because of the enormous volume of the waste. While a family farmer can apply animal waste as organic fertilizer to crops, factory farms have to find other disposal methods.

MILLIONS OF GALLONS

In southwest Utah, for example, 50,000 acres have been set aside for a swine operation with an annual production of 2.5 million hogs. Smithfield Foods, Carroll Foods, Murphy Family Farms and Prestage Farms are collaborating to build this giant hog facility. Instead of being processed in treatment facilities, the waste which could exceed that for all of Los Angeles, will be stored in open-air lagoons notorious for leaks and spills.

Kathryn Hohmann, the Sierra Club director of environment quality, and a former worker on a large hog operation in Kansas, warns, "America's drinking water is at risk. We've seen the product of corporate livestock factories — the waste from thousands of hogs, chickens and cattle — poison water supplies and sicken communities.

NOT JUST A BAD SMELL

Tyson's Foods made headlines in June [1998] for daily dumping thousands of gallons of poultry sludge allegedly containing chicken guts and feathers in a field in Maryland. *The Washington Post* reported that Tyson ignored an April letter from the State of Maryland asking the company to stop applying the sludge.

"The Tyson circumstance is further evidence that the time has come for big poultry companies to take responsibility for the environmental impacts of their operations, not only sludge and wastewater but the manure and dead birds as well," says George Chmael, Maryland staff attorney with the environmental group Chesapeake Bay Foundation. Two months after Maryland told Tyson that it was dumping illegal amounts of chicken waste, and three days after *The Washington Post* reported on the dumping, Tyson announced it was ceasing to dump in the Maryland field.

Tyson representatives say the company acted properly. "The State sent us a letter on April 30 [1998] advising us to find alternative means of disposal," says Ed Nicholson, a Tyson spokesperson. "It takes time to find alternatives and we stopped land application on June 23." Despite requests, Tyson officials failed to provide a copy of the letter.

"*The Washington Post* has taken credit for our decision to find an alternative sludge disposal site," Nicholson says. "In fact, the announcement was coincidental. And as for the reports of chicken feathers and parts, nothing can be further from the truth. These parts are filtered out before application."

Illegal dumping and spills are persistent problems throughout the country. Major hog, chicken and cow waste spills have also been reported in Virginia, Indiana and Arkansas. These spills leach nitrate, antibiotics and heavy metals into soil and water.

In Virginia, Smithfield Foods, Inc., was fined $12.6 million in 1997 for more than 6,900 violations of the Clean Water Act over five years, the largest Clean Water Act fine ever, for dumping excessive levels of hog waste pollutants and phosphorous into the Chesapeake Bay. A federal judge sentenced a former manager of Smithfield's wastewater treatment plants to serve 30 months in prison for polluting waterways, destroying documents and falsifying records.

GROUNDWATER

In Arkansas, sewage from a Tyson's Foods processing plant contaminated groundwater in the town of Green Forest in the 1980s, when Bill Clinton was governor. More than a decade later, nearly 300 miles of streams in northwest Arkansas are still too polluted for swimming because of chicken waste.

On June 21, 1995, a hog waste lagoon in Onslow County broke open and dumped more than 22 million gallons of raw sewage into the New River in North Carolina — more than twice the amount of oil spilled by the Exxon Valdez. The result: a massive fish kill and air pollution problems.

Many of the health consequences of factory farm waste pollution are uncertain, but if *pfiesteria* is any indication, the outlook is not pretty. Maryland residents will never forget the initial reports of the outbreak of the toxic microbe *pfiesteria* on the Chesapeake Bay: the scientist who studied the infected fish and suddenly lost her short-term memory; the crab fishers with open sores on their legs and arms; uncertainties about the fish and Blue Crab harvest from the bay.

Scientists are still trying to understand *pfiesteria*, but it has been linked to pollution from factory chicken farms that crowd the eastern shore of Maryland. Both Perdue and Tyson have giant factory farms near the Chesapeake.

Generally, the big agribusiness companies deny responsibility for the environmental harms of factory farms. "We have always recommended the best management practices for poultry sludge and are now working nutrient management plans into contracts," says Tyson's Nicholson. Asked what contractors should do with the animal waste, he says, "The family farm owns the litter and it is an asset to their farm for fertilizer."

RURAL VITALITY THREATENED

Agribusinesses invade struggling farm communities with promises of bringing new jobs and economic vitality. Instead, these operations wreak havoc on rural economies. Factory farms hit family farms much like Wal-Mart hits Mom and Pop stores. They undersell family farmers by moving product at lower profit margins and using more machinery. Corporate giants, like Tyson, do not buy supplies in local stores like family farmers. Instead they tend to purchase feed and machinery through their own corporate headquarters.

Consider these numbers. In the past 15 years, the number of hogs farms has fallen by nearly three quarters, according to Harkin's staff report. The number of hog producers in Missouri dropped 19 percent between 1994 and 1995. According to Iowa Citizens for Community Improvements, every corporate factory farm replaces ten family farmers and every 12,000 hogs produced by factory farms cost 18 jobs.

CAPITALIST PIGS

...Smithfield-Tar Heel is the largest swine slaughterhouse in the world and the linchpin of North Carolina pork output. Built in 1994, Smithfield ran into opposition from community and environmental groups who saw the mega-slaughterhouse as a threat to the Cape Fear River, to a local aquifer, and as a magnet for even more rapid expansion of pork production in Eastern North Carolina. But Tar Heel, North Carolina, and surrounding Bladen County are among the poorest areas in the state, with the highest levels of unemployment, especially among the African-American and Native American populations. Smithfield offered 4,000 jobs as the big carrot, and called on their political muscle to do the rest....

Stan Goff, "North Carolina's Capitalist Pigs," **RESIST**, December 1998.

The economic benefits of mechanization redound almost entirely to the agribusiness giants. While the average salary of a contract grower is $16,000 a year, the agribusiness companies rake in billions in sales and hundreds of millions in profit. In 1997, the Tyson/Hudson's company reported $6.4 billion in sales, Smithfield Foods registered $3.9 billion and Perdue reported $2.2 billion.

SHARECROPPERS

Water pollution from factory farms poisons local streams and wells, further degrading the quality of rural life. Bill Berry's family has been farming the same piece of land in Oklahoma for three generations. He grew up fishing and swimming in Honey Creek, a stream that flows through his farm. But in the late 1950s, a chicken processing plant was built upstream. The poultry operation has grown into a giant chicken complex that discharges 1.6 million gallons of wastewater per day, much of it leading into Honey Creek. Local drinking water wells have been declared unsafe for human consumption by the State Department of Environmental Quality. No one swims in the creek.

Giant livestock factories effectively turn family farmers into sharecroppers. The corporate units offer the struggling family farmers — weakened further by the entrance of factory farms — a

116

deal. The company offers to supply grain and antibiotics and the animals, and to pay the farms for raising the animals until they are mature. In exchange, the farmer generally takes out a mortgage, builds an animal confinement building and agrees to raise the animals.

The contract growers get a raw deal and, as a result, so does the environment. Although the company owns all live animals on the farm, the contract grower is the legal owner of all the animal waste and all dead animals. The contract grower often cannot even afford mortgage payments and can easily become overburdened with the disposal of animal waste and of animals that succumb to disease — a huge problem with animals living in such close proximity, an arrangement that facilitates the quick spread of disease.

COMMUNITY RESISTANCE

The impact of factory farms on rural communities has inspired a backlash against factory farming and calls to protect the environment from animal waste pollution. Groups like the Missouri Rural Crisis Center, Family Farms for the Future, the Sierra Club and Farm Aid are calling attention to the issue. The Sierra Club and family farmers are now calling for a national moratorium on new factory farms until safeguards are in place to protect water and air.

In a news release, the National Pork Producer Council said that, "Far from helping family farmers 'catch up' with larger, better-capitalized operators, a moratorium would actually put small operators at an even greater disadvantage."

Others in the private sector are more affirmatively seeking to assist family farmers. Ben and Jerry's ice cream company has committed to buy all of its milk and cream from family farms in Vermont. Patchwork Family Farms, the economic development project of the Missouri Rural Crisis Center, offers restaurants and grocery stores pork products produced entirely on family farms.

Bill Berry, the Oklahoma farmer, is fighting back against factory farm pollution. He formed the citizens' group Concerned Citizens for Green Country Conservation. "Those of us who own farms are caretakers of our land," Berry explains. "The streams do not belong to us. They belong to everyone. It is everyone's responsibility to protect our streams and our lands and if we do not, we have failed in life. We do not want to leave it to our heirs and successors to clean up our mess."

PIGNORANCE: FACTORY FARMS AND POLLUTION

Dennis T. Avery

Dennis T. Avery is Director of the Hudson Institute's Center for Global Food Issues. He is editor of Global Food Quarterly *and author of a comprehensive book about saving wildlife through high-yield farming entitled,* Saving the Planet through Pesticides and Plastic: The Environmental Triumph of High-Yield Farming.

■ POINTS TO CONSIDER

1. Describe the trend in meat consumption.

2. List the advantages of modern hog and poultry production, according to Avery.

3. According to Avery, what is the source of the waste that pollutes U.S. rivers?

4. Evaluate the author's contention that "nutrients [in rivers] may not be much of a problem at all."

Dennis T. Avery, "Pignorance," **American Outlook,** Summer 1998. Reprinted with permission of the Hudson Insitute.

If the watchdogs are truly worried about over-fertilized streams, they should be pointing toward cities such as St. Louis and Kansas City....

A list of "America's Most Endangered Rivers" for 1998 flashed across the country recently. The headline ran: "Environmental Group Warns Hog, Chicken Farms Harming U.S. Rivers."

IGNORANCE

A watchdog group called American Rivers put out the list — and a message that "factory hog and chicken farms are a growing national blight on our nation's rivers...so pervasive it could send us back to the days when rivers...were nothing more than cesspools." I hate to say it about nice people who care about cleaning up our rivers, but their crusade could set environmental rescue back a decade. Ignorance won't clean up our rivers.

Even worse, this dislike of big hog farms is betraying the future of the world's forests. The big problem is that the world now has far more people with high incomes, and these people want to eat meat like the rest of us. Globally, meat consumption is rising by five million tons per year. Eventually, world production will expand from its current one billion hogs to about three billion and from the current thirteen billion chickens to perhaps fifty billion.

Traditional small farms have allowed livestock wastes to drain into our streams and rivers for centuries. (I grew up next to a herd of wallowing, rooting hogs in Michigan. Fortunately, they were downstream.) To raise two billion more pigs outdoors, in traditional small herds and flocks, we would have to convert millions of square miles from wildlands to pasture. That land would have to be taken from the world's forests. At four hogs per acre, we would need half the land area of Brazil (1.5 million square miles) just for the extra hogs! And all the urine and manure from these animals would wash into the rivers. It would be an environmental catastrophe.

Fortunately, modern farming is far different. The manure from big, confined hog and poultry houses is an environmental bonus, not a problem. The animal wastes are carefully saved in lagoons, tanks, or dry storage and spread on growing crops. (Organic farmers have been telling Americans for decades that these wastes make the finest, safest fertilizer of all. Modern hog and poultry farms take them up on it.)

FARMS USE NUTRIENTS, CITIES DUMP THEM

When we called the American Rivers office, they told us that each big hog and poultry farm produces as much waste as a small city and pours it into our rivers.

It is true that the wastes from hogs, chickens — and humans — contain large amounts of nitrate and phosphorous, and that these nutrients can overfertilize streams, as mentioned. As noted earlier, however, the big hog and poultry farms don't dump their waste in streams; they collect it and spread it on growing crops. Thus most of their nitrogen turns into plant growth or volatilizes into the air.

If the watchdogs at American Rivers are truly worried about over-fertilized streams, they should be pointing toward cities such as St. Louis and Kansas City that are pouring huge amounts of nutrients into rivers like the Mississippi and Missouri. Unfortunately, they seem to be victims of some terrible misinformation about pollution. Steve Ellis, an American Rivers staffer, told me that his organization does not worry about cities being a nutrient-pollution problem because "the cities treat their wastewater before releasing it."

He seemed unaware that modern urban sewage treatment removes hardly any of the nitrogen and phosphate from wastewater. The Federal Clean Water Act doesn't even class these nutrients as pollutants. Moreover, every rainstorm flushes tons of nitrous oxide from auto exhausts through the storm sewers and into the streams American Rivers says it wants to protect.

FARMS DON'T KILL FISH

American Rivers rates the pretty little Pocomoke River in eastern Maryland as the second-most-endangered river in America — and its staffers blame farmers. American Rivers says that factory poultry farms in the Pocomoke watershed "stimulate the growth of *pfiesteria*...[a parasite] that has been killing fish and making swimmers and boaters ill."

But there's nothing to back up their claim:

- The Maryland Governor's *Pfiesteria* Action Group and a panel of scientists both publicly reported that there is no connection between *pfiesteria* and poultry farming.

FRAGMENTATION AND LAND OWNERSHIP

Continuing fragmentation of land hurts ranching, hunting and wildlife conservation. It is an issue that is common to these groups, and requires a cooperative strategy among them. As 20-acre "ranchettes" replace the traditional ranch, rural activities including ranching and hunting are becoming less a part of the landscape. Fragmented land also makes managing for wildlife throughout the full range of their habitat more difficult....

Dividing up the land also threatens the viability of ecosystems. As a result of development, pasture and grasslands are destroyed, wetlands are filled in, and riparian areas are lost as springs are diverted. Together with the loss of habitat comes the loss of natural forces such as fire and floods that shape the land; worse yet, as natural forces are suppressed, the risk of catastrophic floods and fires increases....

National Cattlemen's Beef Association," Fragmentation of Land Ownership and Its Impact on the Economy and Environment," Englewood, CO: NCBA available at www.beef.org.

- The Pocomoke's poultry farms have moved almost entirely to zero-discharge management in the last dozen years. However, the river has two urban sewage treatment plants, and each releases half a million gallons of wastewater per day.

- One of the three Maryland rivers that had *pfiesteria* outbreaks in 1997 has virtually no chicken farms nearby, and hardly any other such "nutrient sources."

- Scientists believe that high fish populations (or low water volumes) may trigger the toxic attacks by *pfiesteria*.

Number Eight on the American Rivers 1998 endangered list is the Apple River in northern Illinois. The folks at American Rivers assert that the Apple is "threatened by factory hog farms."

True, two of the most modern hog farms in the world are being built in the Apple Valley, but they will not pollute the river. They are designed to save their wastes and use them as organic fertilizer. The operation will also be closely monitored, by both state officials and wary environmentalists such as Steve Ellis. It is far from clear, by contrast, that the sewage treatment plants in the Illinois communities of Woodbine, Elizabeth, and Hanover are protecting the Apple from nutrient pollution.

TESTING THE WATERS?

Actually, nutrients may not be much of a problem at all. We simply don't know. We did not test any of our streams for nutrient levels before 1972, and we haven't done much since. We must also remember that most of the nutrients consumed by fish, frogs, and other marine creatures come from the land. Thus the marine life also needs nitrogen and phosphorus. Streams do need some nitrogen and phosphorus.

It is important to note that American Rivers is trying to gain support for a renewed and expanded Clean Water Act, and the organization is well aware that it took a crisis atmosphere to get the first Clean Water Act passed, in 1972. Today, however, hardly anyone doubts that clean water legislation is correct and necessary. And we have already spent trillions of dollars on sewage treatment and industrial wastewater cleanup.

UNBIASED RESEARCH

If American Rivers really wants to protect America's rivers, it might lobby for a Clean Water Act that requires someone to test the water to find out where we actually have problems! Unfortunately, the current lack of data suits the activists just fine. When no one has good data, the field is wide open for people who write scary press releases.

We deserve clean water regulation based on something more solid than panicky press releases. Unbiased research and a willingness to accept the results are the way to achieve it.

WHAT IS POLITICAL BIAS?

This activity may be used as an individualized study guide for students in libraries and resource centers or as a discussion catalyst in small group and classroom discussions.

Many readers are unaware that written material usually expresses an opinion or bias. The skill to read with insight and understanding requires the ability to detect different kinds of bias. Political bias, race bias, sex bias, ethnocentric bias and religious bias are five basic kinds of opinions expressed in editorials and literature that attempt to persuade. This activity will focus on political bias defined in the glossary below.

Five Kinds of Editorial Opinion or Bias

Sex Bias — the expression of dislike for and/or feeling of superiority over a person because of gender or sexual preference.

Race Bias — the expression of dislike for and/or feeling of superiority over a racial group.

Ethnocentric Bias — the expression of a belief that one's own group, race, religion, culture or nation is superior. Ethnocentric persons judge others by their own standards and values.

Political Bias — the expression of opinions and attitudes about government-related issues on the local, state, national or international level.

Religious Bias — the expression of a religious belief or attitude.

Guidelines

Read through the following statements and decide which ones represent political opinion or bias. Evaluate each statement by using the method indicated below.

---

* **Mark (P)** — *for statements that reflect political opinion or bias.*
* **Mark (F)** — *for any factual statements.*
* **Mark (O)** — *for statements of opinion that reflect other kinds of opinion or bias.*
* **Mark (N)** — *for any statements that you are not sure about.*

What Is Political Bias?: Meat, Environment and Ethics

_____1.   The fact in modern agribusiness is that we kill animals, birds and fish in such numbers that we dare not think too much about it. In addition, we mistreat the animals from the day they are born until the day we kill them, so that we can eat them cheaply and so that armies of middlepersons can get rich off the transactions.

_____2.   As personal income grows, the diets of individuals contain more high quality and expensive food, including more meat. Economic globalization created middle classes of people in nations only known, formerly, for abject poverty. These new middle classes, as the premise suggests, are demanding higher quality food and more meat.

_____3.   The fast food diet of the First World is gaining popularity in less developed countries. Fast food chains, particularly American ones, are exporting franchises to nations such as China. Kentucky Fried Chicken was among the first U.S. chains to enter China, opening its first store in 1987. It now has more than 280 locations in 65 cities across China.[1] The consequences of the high-fat, high-calorie diet in the First World are tremendous. Five hundred thousand Americans die of cancer every year. But the consequences of this type of diet in the Third World will be even greater, for these nations do not have the high-tech health care system to deal with the effects of chronic illnesses brought on by a gluttonous, First World diet.

_____4.   No society has ever been voluntarily vegetarian. This means that the increase in demand observed in the consumption of meat is not likely reversible. Hence, if farmers must produce more meat, the best means to do so is through more efficient production which consumes less land which is now wildlife habitat.

_____5.   One hundred thousand cattle are slaughtered every 24 hours in the U.S.[2]

_____6.   Cattle eat most of the grain produced on earth. A relatively new trend, from forage to feed, has progressed in this century with little discussion of the consequences for the environment or food distribution.

_____7.   People in power have always eaten meat. Women historically, as second-class citizens, have eaten what is considered to be second-class food — namely vegetables and grains. The sexism of meat eating is delineated by a mythology that permeates all classes. Meat eating is a constant male activity and an intermittent activity for women. This trend is painfully observed in famine-stricken nations today.[3]

[1] "Fast Food, Western Colas Highlight China Growth," **National Catholic Reporter,** 29 January 1999.

[2] Rifkin, Jeremy, "Beyond Beef," **Utne Reader,** March/April 1992.

[3] Adams, Carol, "The Sexual Politics of Meat," **Utne Reader,** March/April 1992.

BIBLIOGRAPHY

Avery, Dennis T. **Biodiversity: Saving Species with Biotechnology,** Indianapolis: Hudson Institute, 1993.

Avery, Dennis T., **Saving the Planet with Pesticides and Plastic: The Environmental Triumph of High-Yield Farming,** Indianapolis: Hudson Institute, 1995.

Brown, Lester, et al., **Beyond Malthus: Sixteen Dimensions of the Population Problem,** Washington, D.C.: Worldwatch Institute, 1998.

Dasgupta, Biplab, **Structural Adjustment, Global Trade and the New Political Economy of Development,** London: Zed Books, 1998.

Fifty Years Is Enough: The Case Against the World Bank and the International Monetary Fund, Kevin Danaher, ed., Boston: South End Press, 1994.

Hunger and Public Action, Jean Dreze and Amartya Sen, eds., Oxford: Clarendon Press, 1989.

Killick, Tony, **Aid and the Political Economy of Political Change,** London: Routledge, 1998.

Lipton, Michael, **New Seeds and Poor People,** Baltimore: Johns Hopkins University Press, 1989.

Malthus, Thomas Robert, **An Essay on the Principle of Population,** New York: Oxford University Press, 1993.

Neurath, Paul, **From Malthus to the Club of Rome and Back,** Armonk, NY: ME Sharpe, 1994.

Norman Borlaug on Hunger, Anwar Dil, ed., San Diego: Intercultural Forum, 1997.

The Political Economy of Hunger: Selected Essays, Jean Dreze, et al., eds., New York: Oxford University Press, 1995.

Rifkin, Jeremy, **The Biotech Century: Harnessing the Gene and Remaking the World,** New York: Putnam, 1998.

Sen, Amartya, **Poverty and Famines: An Essay on Entitlement and Deprivation,** New York: Oxford University Press, 1981.

Online Resources

Alliance for Sustainability – www.mtn.org/iasa/

Bread for the World – www.bread.org/

The Center for Global Food Issues – www.hudson.org/

The Institute for Food and Development Policy (Food First)
www.foodfirst.org/

The International Monetary Fund – www.imf.org/

Jubilee 2000 – www.jubilee2000uk.org/

Organic Farming Research Foundation – www.ofrf.org/

The United Nations Food and Agriculture Organization
www.fao.org/

INDEX